The God Code

—

We Are Robots!

Also by Steve Rhodes

The Prophecy of Ra Uru Hu

Steve Rhodes

The God Code

We Are Robots!

RME
LONDON
baantu.com

First published 2017 by
RME
London
United Kingdom

First Edition (rev. 1.21)
Copyright © 2017 by Steve Rhodes
Steve Rhodes asserts the moral right to be
identified as the author of this work.

ISBN 978 1 9735418 5 1

Editor: Stephanie Sprague

Visit **baantu.com** to find more out about the author and any news.

Disclaimer:

"All relationships,
even the long lasting ones,
are impossible."

INTRODUCTION

There are things inside of us that are as old as the universe. They come from the Bhan. The Bhan was never alive, yet it carried the building plan for all life.

You think you are in control of your life? You are not. The gods are. The Bhan shattered into countless pieces at the Big Bang – into a number so big it can't be imagined. These are your gods. The Bhan and its shattered aspects aren't alive. We are. The Bhan can't think. We can. Every life form, every tree, every fish, every bird, every insect, mammal, and human carries two Bhan aspects. But the vast majority of Bhans will never incarnate into forms. Instead of building physical forms, they are the builders of consciousness. All Bhans communicate with the help of neutrinos. Without the Bhans, there wouldn't be life. Without them, there would be chaos.

The universe is a living being and you are inside of it. Now, imagine all the cells within your own body. They are in a similar situation as yourself. They have no clue what's going on. They don't know what a human body is, let alone that there are billions of humans out there in an even larger unknown world.

Life is like matryoshka dolls, the Russian dolls nested

within each other. There's always another layer underneath and above. It's all about scale.

We are the only life-form that has a mind. This is both a blessing and a curse at the same time. It makes us the only living thing in the universe aware of our own existence, while our strategic capacity and greed has put us at the top of the food chain. But the awareness of our own existence or self-reflective consciousness also has the unpleasant side-effect: We know one day we will be annihilated. We have rather amusing and irrational ways to deal with this little problem. Aware of our own demise, we try to get even more done in the time we have in the bizarre assumption that a "fulfilled" and "long" life makes dying easier or more justified. Another interesting way is our fairy tale of heaven and the afterlife.

Some humans are obsessed with science and logic, but I don't see much of that in their daily lives. I used to make fun of them, but no more. Because no matter how logical and rational you think you are, you can never really figure out or know what's going on. Hope is often very important to people. So robbing them of it, without giving them a replacement to make their lives bearable, is not doing anyone a service.

I spent my childhood years in a boarding school inside the famous Melk Abbey, a Benedictine abbey on a rocky outcrop overlooking the Danube river and the Wachau valley in Austria. When I came out of it, and in spite of the fact I liked it there, I quit the Catholic church, which is not something people in Austria do lightly. Later, I studied at university, and was tortured with maths for probability, yet it suited my now nihilistic mind that embraced the chaos theory of life. Instead of Jesus, I became a worshipper of the Gaussian Curve.

Of course, when you are in your early '20s, you think death is an eternity away. It happens to others, but won't to you. So why even think about it? And you're still carrying the illusion your life can be *anything* you want it to be. Hope is a great aphrodisiac. The American Dream and God are both built on a lie. But they provide hope. And hope is everything.

What happened in the next 30 years that followed had nothing to do with statistics, random events, God, or what I wanted in life. I had, and still have, a colourful life. I've seen and experienced extreme highs and lows. I have been with people from all walks of life from the super-famous to the dirt-poor nobodies to everyone in between.

When I say that my life had nothing to do with random events, here's an example. I arrived in London in the late '90s. I didn't know anyone, yet was absolutely certain and convinced of an eventual iconic career in the music business. I had this wish to work with the same people who my idols had worked with and thought this is the only reason I still hadn't made it myself.

London is a city of more than 10 million people during the day and the chance of meeting someone from this small, elite club are almost nonexistent. I was an absolute nobody in London when I arrived, with nothing to my name. Only a few had access to the internet back then, email was relatively new and social media, YouTube and reality TV were totally unheard of and not invented yet.

The only person I knew was a young music instrument dealer. He had just opened his own tiny shop on the outskirts of London, which wasn't much more than a little room serving as an office. He sold me a pair of speakers for my little studio at home. One day he called and asked if he could come around with someone who would like to check out my speakers. Fifteen minutes later, one of the guys I had always wanted to meet (from that small, elite circle of people working with one of my idols) was standing in my room, listening to my music. I didn't do anything and yet it happened. What are the chances of that?

A few months later, a new genre of music emerged in London and I was totally into it. I too recorded a new song in that genre, which I thought for sure could be my stepping stone into the London music scene. Now for six months I had a record from one of the most successful artists in the same genre sitting on my desk. He was a Londoner and his debut album number one in the charts. Rumour had it, he had been given a one-million-pound contract by a major record company. I wanted to be him!

Again, back then remember the internet didn't exist the way it does now. There was no eBay either. When you had something to sell, you had to advertise it in the "Loot", a paper for second-hand sales. So one day I was waiting for somebody to come around and pick up an item I had for sale. When the doorbell rang, I could see through my small, round window who was outside. He reminded me of the guy on the record sitting on my desk. Of course such a thing would be ridiculous, so I gave him what he wanted, not mentioning that I was a musician. As he was about to leave he said: "What is it that you do, Steve?"

Reluctantly (I thought he was a time-waster) I told him that I'm a musician. He (of course) replied that he is one too and just got this deal with a major record company. I was dizzy. This can't be happening again! Sure enough, it was the famous guy from the record. He took my song and the next day played it on BBC Radio where he had a presenter slot.

Things like that kept happening in the next few years. For instance, a few years ago, after a long break, I recorded a few songs and was researching which record companies I could send it to, in order to get some feedback. I had a list of people from the UK, but was wondering if I could find a few from the US. After a bit of research I came across a guy named Martin Kierszenbaum, who had quite an impressive track record and was largely responsible for the success of Lady Gaga. Of course there was no way for me to reach such a big player from America. The next day, I went past the empty reception of the building where I have my little studio in London, and when the door bell rang, I did something which I usually never do (I have my own door bell for my studio). I went behind that reception desk, picked up the receiver of the intercom, asking "Who is it?". The reply was: "Martin Kierszenbaum". I laughed out loud after hanging up. My first thought was that I was going slightly insane.

You need to know I had never met one record-company executive in our building in ten years, and even if there might have been one, he surely hadn't been from the US. So when I heard his name, I assumed I must have misheard and this is just the usual food delivery for one of the other residents. But my curiosity was tickled, so after buzzing him in, I waited at reception. A black limo with a driver arrived and a guy stepped out of the car walking towards me. I asked him if he was Martin from Interscope Records, and indeed he was.

And no, it's not like I became super-successful or famous or anything like that. What happened in my life did not exactly dovetail with my wishes and what I wanted. That's not why I'm telling you this. Rather, I want to emphasise the fact that these things can't happen if you believe in a random universe or how most of us logically try to understand it.

There is no chaos. There is order. But who is responsible for it? My attitude changed after several of these incidences. We commonly divide the world into believers and nonbelievers, which is totally stupid. The first group believes in things almost religiously, although there is no evidence of their existence, while the other group is convinced that things don't exist, unless they see them, touch them or experience them. Both of them have zero proof for what they are saying. After my experiences, when arriving in London, which I couldn't explain, I didn't belong in any of these two categories any more. My new motto was: "There are many things out there that exist, but I have no clue about them." I became open-minded, but not a believer. I knew there were things in existence that the world hadn't taught me. But I also noticed different things happen to different people. And they are not random. Our lives are truly unique. We have a unique purpose. We all have our own stories.

Everything we can know and understand is just a theory. Which means we know nothing with absolute certainty. It doesn't matter if your name is Einstein, Hawking, or Rhodes. Some theories might be more convincing than others, but eventually they all break down. The concept of scientific proof is nothing but an experiment that can predict the outcome to a certain degree. Nothing is bullet proof and neither is it necessarily a truthful explanation.

We might trust things "clever" people tell us, but also trust and rely on conclusions we draw ourselves. There is never absolute proof for any of it. Think about the actual difference between science and religion. There isn't much. They both give us comfort or in their own ways offer help to make our lives easier, but in the end, we all die and none of us the wiser about why we were here. We have no real idea what is going on.

If you go back to the story about the cells within our bodies, they have no clue what they are doing either. So how can they even be in the right place at the right time, doing whatever it is they must do to keep us alive? And then there is this incredible level of violence in the cellular domain. If all cells were peaceful, we would be all dead. You can't run life based on morality. But how can anything get done if neither the cells nor any of us know what life is about?

My theory is that there is an invisible *Program*. Scientists tell us that only 4.9% of the universe is ordinary matter, which we can see. The rest is dark matter, dark energy and neutrinos – basically fancy words for "we don't know what it is, but it's out there". Imagine that dark matter is the intelligence or "software" of the universe. It is the building plan. Neutrinos are the pathways connecting it all together. They move information at almost the speed of light in any direction, going through everything in a straight line. They are produced in stars and have tiny amounts of matter. The Bhan is dark matter and not alive. It only changes the information of the neutrinos, similar to a prism changing light that passes through it. It is the mechanism influencing everything that is alive. How do you think birds know where to fly for winter and summer? There is no such thing as "instinct". There is only the Program. "Instinct" is just another word for "we know we should do it, but don't know why". I started this book by saying each of us carry this Bhan within us, but in fact we carry two aspects of Bhan dark matter. They are both organisers responsible for the influence on not just the body, but the mind and love. If you want to know the details about the Bhan, I recommend you read my other book *The Prophecy of Ra Uru Hu*.

The latest buzz words in the tech world are A.I. and machine learning. What it means is that we give machines or computers a certain level of autonomy so they can solve problems on their own, but also teach themselves. They can learn without being explicitly programmed. This is different from the classic step-by-step rules, created by programmers, they had to follow in the past. What never occurs to us is that we function in the same way. We are nothing but intelligent machines or robots that are controlled by a larger Program. But the Program is not alive or aware of what it's doing either. It's not an old man with white hair and a beard. It doesn't come from a central or higher place.

There exists a certain level of autonomy for us – you can call it improvisation – which humans understand as free will. But the Program through the Bhan controls the larger outline of what it wants us to do and intervenes when necessary. This is similar to how we deal with children. You establish boundaries with them, and inside of those boundaries they can do whatever they want. That allows you to have your own life, too – otherwise you would have to watch them all the time, which would be terribly inefficient. You can also give them a goal or task and they figure out for themselves how to do it.

It's exactly how life controls us, or on a deeper level, the cells within us. How does a cell know it has to be inside the knee and not the brain? It doesn't, but the Program makes it. It creates order out of chaos. It organises all life within the universe in a particular pattern, like a beautiful dance.

The Program influences us through certain traits that we possess. We are also programmed to favour certain qualities in other people. It's not about loving and liking *everyone* (which isn't possible) or everyone liking and loving you, but rather about seeing it as an indication about where you belong. It's not about *general* judgment, but *individual*. There is no universally good or bad person.

Neither is there a right nor wrong person that we can all agree upon in some universal way. There are no universal definitions for so many of these judgment calls that most people make all day long, day after day. The same goes for anything you do in your life, including your diet and what you eat. We are all different and we have different tasks and needs. Nobody on this planet knows what's best for you except *you*.

People always think they are lost, which makes them easy prey for self-help systems, books and all kind of New Age practices and self-proclaimed gurus. We have always been told that we are flawed, that we are sinners, that we are imperfect from the moment we were born. But what all these forms of "help" do is actually take away our own authority and power (and money). The truth is that we are all lost, but at the same time we aren't. Just because we can't know what's going on, doesn't mean we are lost.

My book is not a self-help book. It is a way to let you see what the Program wants from you, how it influences and supports you. This book helps you to recognise your essential nature so you might get rid of the incorrect fantasy that might have been planted about who you "think" you are, or what you "could" become instead of who you are.

But here comes the important bit: Just because you might know more about your nature and who you actually are doesn't mean you get the life you want. It's not just about you, but about the larger thing that you are within. Most of us are ignorant about the fact that we belong to a larger living organism. No matter what you think, it's the Program, which is in charge of many aspects. It rules your life and controls what's possible or not.

At the same time, we do have autonomy, we can improvise. Our lives are the sum total of the influences coming from the Bhan as well as the things happening in our lives. We learn from our experiences and become more intelligent beings. We do this through our autonomy and improvisation. It's not like our whole life is scripted. Only certain things are.

I've spent the last 15 years trying to understand parts of the Program and how we can decipher it. I was a computer geek and a coder as teenager before entering the music business. When the music biz spit me out at the other end, I began to develop a software that would allow me to see the influences of the Program.

I called it *BaanTu*.

THE GRAPH

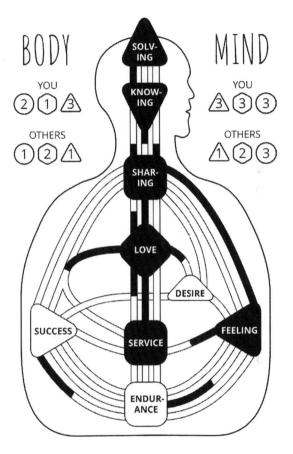

This is a condensed graphical representation of the Program that's influencing you, me and every other human being. What you see here is my own *Graph*. If you would like to calculate yours or someone else's, then go to my web site **baantu.com** where you can register a free account that allows you to create Graphs. You'll also have access to the Graphs of more than 1,000 famous people, including writers, artists, politicians, and musicians, not to mention sports stars, movie stars, and celebrities.

In order to calculate a Graph, you need a very precise birth time. Many of us have a birth time marked on our birth certificate. If you don't see it on yours, you might be able to call the issuing authority or the hospital where you were born. The BaanTu software can show you when the Graph begins to change, earlier or later from the time you've entered. You must expect changes at least every 76 minutes. They can range from subtle to dramatic. If you have no time at all, I don't recommend calculating a Graph. There are too many fundamental changes throughout a day.

BaanTu is not related to the Chakra energy system, despite its similar looking Graph with its centres. It's also not related to the ancient I-Ching, despite the use of the 64 Hexagrams in the Mandala Wheel used for the calculation (press the "Wheel" button in the **baantu.com** software to see it). It's neither related to Kabbalah nor to astrology, despite using the positions of the 13 celestial bodies in our solar system for its calculation. I would not recommend mixing up any knowledge coming from those fields with BaanTu.

*

BaanTu reveals the influence of the Program that becomes part of your nature. It also shows the kind of people who interest you. One of its most amazing features shows what kind of relationship you have with others and how much time you are comfortable spending with them. Every relationship has four basic components that BaanTu can see:

+ How attractive you find the other's qualities.
+ How compatible you are.
+ How much you motivate each other to do things.
+ How much you dominate each other.

BAANTU

If BaanTu is not a self-help system, then what is it? The phrase "self-help" system is an oxymoron. It suggests that you are able to help yourself, but only with somebody else telling you what to do and often with their own set of rules and instructions for you to follow.

Instead, BaanTu is a mirror. It allows you to see your nature better. When you look in an actual mirror, it only reflects your physical appearance. It doesn't give you opinions on how you look, or suggest how to cut your hair or any instructions on how to wash your face. The only talking-mirrors are in fairy tales. BaanTu doesn't come with opinions and instructions.

There are no two human beings on this planet who are the same. Every person has a slightly different task and we all have unique physical bodies with a unique DNA. Everything in life, at least at a certain level, is unique. This means that neither myself nor anybody else can ever totally know you or be certain about what's "good" for you – not even the universe itself. And the universe *is* God. Did you ever imagine that you are inside of God?

Don't get carried away. God's will is the Program. It's the consciousness created by all the Bhan Crystals and the neutrinos. It's the Program that is in control of what happens. Wouldn't it be nice to see a little bit more clearly what the damn Program wants?

No matter what you might think now, BaanTu is not here to guarantee you a better life. No system or *general* guidance can. You are a unique individual and therefore must make a unique decision. It's not that other people or BaanTu can't be of help. It's about recognising that *you* are in control and responsible for the decisions you make. But also realize you are not alone with that task. The Program has an interest in you, because the universe needs you. It will give you all the help you need. Everything is connected. You are never alone. So don't despair. Most people are only in despair because they didn't get what they wanted. Don't make the same mistake. You go through life to discover what the universe (Program) wants. Then you must deal with all the challenges along that way to the best of your abilities. And at times life hurts and at other times it's wonderful. That's what life is. Not everything in life can be changed and pain is an essential part of it.

If BaanTu shows you have a difficult relationship with someone, it won't tell you to avoid that person. You will automatically spend less time with that person anyway. There isn't much to "do".

If the Graph shows your judgment in life is "Feeling",

it won't come with any instructions. There is nothing to do with that information. It's already happening. BaanTu is a mirror that lets you see with more clarity why things in your life are happening the way they do. But most importantly, it can reveal why you are different from other people and in what ways.

Another important point to understand is that the Program doesn't stand still and neither do you. You will always see changes in your Graph and others. You will see you are never the same all the time. On some days you are more motivated to do certain things more than other days and vice versa. Have you not noticed? It's what we call *Transit* in BaanTu and you can see it by pressing the *Trans* button under the Graph. Or you can press the period buttons under the profile picture for *48 h, week, month,* or *1/2 year,* which will automatically change your "motivation" meters and the activations in the Graph.

Do you have any idea how many people pray every day in the hope God speaks to them? If God doesn't speak to you, the Graph might be the next best thing. I always tell people to pay attention to what their life is telling them instead of listening to self-help books or gurus. Yes, life speaks to you! It gives you signs. It speaks to you through your environment, but also from your inside. But you might miss them when you are staring at your smart phone and all the comments and opinions of other people who have nothing to do with you or your life. Even if they have millions of followers, they don't really know what's best for you. It means nothing. Why not be the main actor in your own reality show – your own life? Why not be smart and take responsibility for your own life? Blindly following others, who aren't even part of your life isn't always smart. You have all the information you need to make the right decision on your own, and sometimes that might just be a "feeling", not even something rational.

BODY & MIND

In the Graph, there are separate influences for body and mind. The reason for this is, again, we have two Bhan aspects within us. One is controlling the body, the other the mind. Before we can even begin looking at the influence of the Program, we must be clear what these two words *mind* and *body* mean in the context of BaanTu.

Traits that fall into the mind category are aspects of the Program that influence the way you *use your mind*, which includes thinking, speaking, watching, communicating, memorising and learning, but also how you judge. It also influences what kind of ideas you have that shape your goals. It gives us an insight into *why* you are doing what you do in the particular way you do.

The *body* side is everything else that the mind is not. But most of all it's an influence for *using our bodies*. Essentially, it's about what we do with them, but also about anything concerning the material plane. The mind programming might have an idea, but it depends upon the body how we execute it. Most of what we do in life is a composite of mind and body. The mind (also called your *Personality* in BaanTu) is usually in control (it has an idea), but must acknowledge the way of the body in terms of what it is capable and confident to do, including its limitations. For example, the body might be uncomfortable or afraid of making contact with strangers. If the mind has an idea, the body might feel more comfortable working with the people it already knows instead of taking risks with strangers. Of course, the mind becomes aware of the body's discomfort and will take it into account in the future. That's how it learns.

We will get to all these nuances, so you can see for yourself what the Program does to *you*. To get a first taste of it, go to **baantu.com** and look at the [EASY] page, which is the one you see after your register and log in. When you are done reading the text, switch the [EASY] switch to [GRAPH].

The Program might make you a very confident speaker through the *mind* influence, not afraid of difficult arguments, but at the same time it might make you physically shy and afraid of doing dangerous things or meeting other people through the *body* influence. Everything in our nature is divided into body and mind. It's an incorrect assumption by society to think that a confident person is confident with *both* body and mind. They could be polar opposites, because they come from two different places (the two Bhans). Not many of us are aware of that.

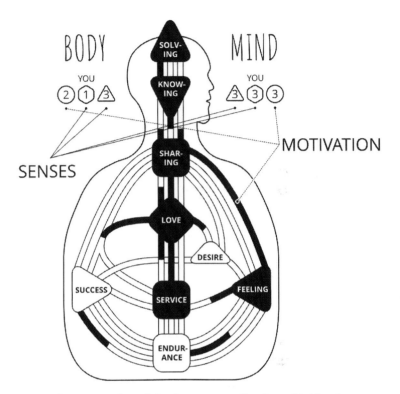

A part from *mind* and *body*, we can further divide the influence of the Program into *senses* and *motivation*. The Triangles and Hexagons represent the sensing influence and show us how we judge. The Circles and the Channels show our motivations, which are largely responsible for our actions. Of course, our senses will also influence our actions. You have to see them as an added nuance to what we have to do. The senses measure our "discomfort". The senses are also responsible for something we call "happiness", which is overrated, but still important.

Many people have the false idea one can have more or less happiness in life. Happiness, pleasure and pain are created by our minds. Pleasure and pain are not absolutes connected to things in life. In fact, each of us all have an equal amount of pain and pleasure.

If you were to look at your whole life and divide it in a "good" and "bad" half, you would have your "pain" and "pleasure". Whatever happens in your life would belong to the "better" or "worse" half. Whatever you would change in your life, you would still have equal halves of pain and pleasure (with various degrees). And so does everyone else, regardless of wealth, fame or fortune. Next time you're jealous, remember. The only difference is that different things are responsible for another's pain and pleasure and yours.

Pain and pleasure, or what is called happiness, is a tool by the Program to control you. It's like the carrot dangling on a stick in front of the donkey.

You have to rise above the illusion that you can have more of one and less of the other. They are both a necessity of life. It's the most important tool the Program has to tell you what to do and where to go. So, yes, it's important to do things that make one happy, but it's not about having *more* happiness in life.

THE THREE SYMBOLS

Any of the three symbols in the Graph have three possible themes, which means you will see numbers between 1-3 inside of them.

Every person has two sets of Triangles, Hexagons and Circles (one set on the mind side and one on the body), describing their own nature in the row marked "you". The row "others" tells us what kind of people they like.

Initially, you might assume there are 729 possible combinations when looking at the six symbols for your own nature. But due to how the Program works, there are actually only 114 possible combinations that exist. For example, it's never possible to have the same number in the Circle for body and mind. Another example is that if someone has a Circle-3 on the mind and Circle-2 on the body, then they must have a Hexagon-3 on the mind and a Hexagon-1 on the body. That's just how the underlying mechanism of the Program works. It only allows certain types in the world.

The three symbols stand for:

Triangle:	Priority (judgment)
Hexagon:	Confidence (resilience)
Circle:	Interaction Type

Don't forget that the three symbols on the mind side influence anything that you are using *your* mind for and the symbols on the body side influence anything that you are using *your* body for. It is not connected to other people's mind and body. It's about your own.

PRIORITY

To the left and right of the head on the Graph are Triangles under "you". For now, we will ignore "others". The influence of the Program can be divided into two groups. The first group consists of the Triangle and Hexagon, measuring what is happening to you. They are your senses and responsible for your judgment of "good" and "bad" or being "happy" or "miserable", although most of the time it's something in-between. They determine your mood through various levels of pain and pleasure. The Triangles and Hexagons act like sensors, judging everything happening in your life and defining your comfort-zone.

The second group of influence consists of the Circles and the nine Pressure Centres inside the human shape. They show us your motivation and interaction types. The numbers inside all three symbols (Triangle, Hexagon, Circle) are responsible for parts of your nature that never change throughout your life. On the other hand, the

Pressure Centres, the themes of your motivation, change all the time.

Let's begin with the Triangles and what they tell. You can think of them as the thing that makes you happy or hurts you. Interestingly, for other people meeting you, it's not always the first thing they see. They usually notice the motivation and interaction types first. Only when they get to know you better, do they understand what controls your mood and how easily you might feel hurt.

We have three different kinds of judgment responsible for your mood (Triangles). They are represented by the numbers 1-2-3.

Whatever your number is within the Triangle, the theme of what that number represents will always be more important to you than the theme the other two numbers represent. If you have a choice, this is what you will go for, because it makes you happy. If your theme is *Feeling*, it means *how you feel* has priority over *Success* or *Respect*.

Possible Themes:

1 – Success
2 – Respect
3 – Feeling

SUCCESS

The theme of *Success* is a broad description of any activity that allows you to succeed in life, to be more secure, or to be better off in life. These people can be quite competitive, no matter if it's with others or themselves. They want to win and achieve their goals at any cost. They can be hard working and disciplined. They love difficult challenges.

The Triangles reveal, out the of the three available themes, what makes you happy or miserable. They control your mood. Anyone with Success has the natural capacity to endure sacrifices in order to succeed, because *Feeling* is not a priority. It doesn't mean these people never care about how they feel, but they have the capacity to ignore it.

You can see people from all walks of life with this: Sports, politics or business. Many of them put their career before other needs or their emotional well-being. It's not a choice for them. It's something the Program insists upon them. They can show excellent control over their emotions in order to be successful. They can easily switch them off when it suits them. Compared with Feeling people, they can look colder, showing less empathy in certain situations. But they *do* have feelings. They just react less to them.

Every aspect we are going to discuss in this book can have "good" and "bad" sides. You must understand that what is considered "good" by some is seen as "bad" by others. Again, the definition of a universal "good" is a myth. It doesn't exist. If you try to be a "good" person, you will still offend someone. What I'm saying is what might sound "horrible" to you, could be seen as something positive by others. BaanTu is not about judging people and labelling them with "good" or "bad", but showing you "why" they do what they do.

For example, there are people with the Triangle-1 who might give the impression to *Respect* (Triangle-2) people that they "prostitute" themselves, because 2's really worry about what other people think. A Triangle-1 is always ready to do things that are unpleasant and sometimes even bad for their image in order to succeed in life. What one person calls "prostitution" could also be seen by others as "making a good effort" or "doing whatever is necessary to succeed". I'm not saying that all Triangle-1 people are prostitutes, but even if somebody were, you can see why they are able to do what they do. They care less about what other people think, regardless if they are respected, and instead are adept at doing "unpleasant" things to become better off in life.

First, we must differentiate whether you have the Triangle-1 theme on the body or mind side. If you have Success on the *mind* side, then everything you use your mind for, everything you talk about, everything you learn or watch or think about is motivated by the need to be successful. The Triangle is measuring how much of the Success theme you get with any mental activity. It judges. If you don't succeed with the things you use your mind for, you begin to feel miserable. Therefore, you don't have much patience for things, people or situations that don't show any prospect of improving your life. If a mental activity doesn't have a practical value to make your life better, you are not happy, you don't want to continue. The obvious (but not only) examples are: Making more money, having more things, winning in a competition, having a better job, getting promoted, succeeding with a business, having a "comfortable" life. One could say that people like this are more goal-orientated and think less about how they feel or what other people say about them. When they make a lot of money, they don't have to tell everyone about it (like the Triangle-2 would) in order to be happy.

When we look at that theme for the *body* side (you could have Triangle-1 on both sides, just one or none), we are talking about any *physical* activity. Here, it's about *doing* and not about using your mind (speaking, thinking, memorising or watching). It's about anything you use your body for or anything that affects your body. An important physical (body) aspect that might not be obvious right away is what kind of people you'd like to meet and what kind of places you'd like to go.

The mind might have an idea *what* you should do, but it's the body side that determines *how* you actually will put your ideas into action. It's an additional quality from that of the mind.

All three themes can have their own specific health problems as well as advantages for different reasons. Don't think one is better than the other. Some might argue the Success person could sacrifice their health more because it wants to succeed, but the other two groups have their own pitfalls, too. Yes, this one might sacrifice its health in order to succeed. It might be for financial reasons or just for the satisfaction to win a sport competition. At the same time, they could look after their health for the very same reasons if they realise a healthy body is more likely to be successful.

There is no group *generally* healthier than the others, although group 3 (the "feel good" group) have a tendency to gain weight more easily, because they don't see the point of suffering (being hungry) for their image or to be successful.

Now go to **baantu.com** and look at a few people you know to find your own examples of how a Triangle-1 is influencing them.

RESPECT

When you closely look at the Triangles at **baantu.com**, you'll see a little dot. It indicates the affected area in the Graph. The Triangle-1 points to Success, Triangle-3 to Feeling, and Triangle-2 to Knowing. When you connect these three Pressure Centres in the Graph with imaginary lines, they form a triangle.

Respect is connected to the mind. The mind is all about judgment. It doesn't know an absolute. All it can do is compare two or more things. If you show it one thing in isolation, it has no opinion. All of a sudden, you realise everything the mind knows is relative to something else only. It doesn't know an absolute truth.

The reason why the Triangle-2 is connected to the mind is because it measures through mental judgment, but it is about judgment coming from *others*. Somebody with this theme cares deeply about what others think about them, but most of all they want to be respected by others.

There are many ways to be respected. Don't jump to narrow conclusions. First of all, you can be respected for your work, knowledge or abilities. Another way would be to create a fake facade or image so people think well about you. I know a few Triangle-2's who are great liars or they hide things that don't look too favourably on them. Then there are Triangle-2's who force people to respect them out of a position of power. As always, there are "good" and "bad" examples.

You will find many actors with the Triangle-2. When somebody craves applause, what do you think this is? It's the theme of this Triangle-2. It's recognition by the audience, it's praise, it's a flattering judgment that makes such a person happy. But they also can be really miserable if they are not respected by others. Because it's the thing that makes them happy, they will always try to favour things that earn them respect. It's not a coincidence that "to put on an act" stands for "lying". There is a similarity between acting and lying. They are both hiding something or pretending. An actor hides who he really is. He is playing a role. And why is he doing it? He's doing it to get the intended reaction from another person. A Triangle-2 doesn't see the point of acting if there is no audience. You must understand that if a Triangle-2 person can't show someone their achievements or possessions, they are pointless. Some of them love to boast about their achievements and can turn into real show-offs. How far you go with this can be connected to your level of insecurity, which we will see in the Hexagon chapter.

Of course, as always, it makes a difference if you have this theme on the mind or the body side.

On the mind side, we are dealing with every activity making use of the mind. It means when you speak or share what you know, you are looking to get the respect of the audience. It also means you only want to learn things that can earn you respect from others. It's not enough that *you* like it. You often need the praise from others that you are good with something. Of course the mind is also responsible for ideas. Anything making you look favourable in other people's eyes is a "good" idea.

It's not enough for such a person to succeed with something and have lots of money and yet nobody knowing about it. If such a person had to choose between being poorer or disrespected by their community, they would probably rather be poorer.

If we look at the body side, we already know it has to do with activities using the body, but also affecting the body. It goes without saying it can be very important for a body Triangle-2 how they look. Every person has different ways to live out the Respect theme. Some do it visually, by trying to look "good", or having a "good" image. Others *demand* Respect out of a position of power. It doesn't matter if you are a dictator, monarch or powerful owner of a business. There are so many ways how Respect can be put into action, but they all have the same motivation: They want to be held in high regard by other people, they want to be judged with esteem and be revered.

There are actors who have the Triangle-2 on the mind and/or on the body side. If they have it on the mind side, their motivation might be to learn a difficult role or character part in order to earn respect from the audience. This makes them happy and is the motivation for all the hard and sometimes painful role study or even training to become an actor. We all know that becoming an actor is no guarantee for success or financial rewards. A Triangle-2 can do it, because this is not the most important thing for them. They primarily want to be held in high esteem or respected by others for what they do. If an actor has this on the body side, it's also about how they look. They can make a great effort to look young and beautiful through physical training, cosmetic surgery or strict diets.

Don't forget to look at what the Triangle-2 is not: It's not about "feeling good" like the 3, so it *can* make sacrifices. And it's not enough to be successful alone. The Triangle-2 needs an audience to be judged. It is always aware of the effect it has on others, which is the prime cause for misery or happiness in its life.

Apart from actors, you'll also find this theme in many dancers and a few musicians, but also in many other skilled professions. Although the most common theme for musician (especially songwriters) is Feeling, Respect can be a strong motivation to become a master of an instrument. Take Al Di Meola, a guitar virtuoso who is technically one of the best in the world. He has a double Triangle-2. To reach that level of skill requires hard training and sacrifices, something the Triangle-3 person struggles with. What makes Di Meola happy and spurs him on is probably the praise from an audience.

Another version of Respect could be to be "feared" by others. It's the "darker brother" of Respect. Benito Mussolini had a double Respect theme.

The theme of the Triangle-2 can be expressed in many ways. Again, check out the people you know or some of the celebrities on **baantu.com** with that theme to get a better understanding of it, and to find your own examples. The best way to learn and understand any of the Program influences is by studying people you know well. For example, what would be a common beginner mistake is to assume only Triangle-2's have cosmetic surgery. Anyone could. Maybe the Triangle-2's have a slightly higher motivation, but what BaanTu tells us is the reason *why* people do what they do. You could have cosmetic surgery for three reasons according to BaanTu: You want to be successful, admired or feel good about yourself. Or maybe you cover up an insecurity (low Hexagon).

FEELING

This theme forces some of us to prioritise our *emotional well-being* (feelings) over the more serious looking themes of Success or Respect.

Feeling is short for "feel good". This is the most important thing in life for these people. They primarily want to enjoy themselves. It's what makes them happy. Everything else comes second. This theme was a very late addition to the Program. Yes, not just your computer and phone get updates, but the universal life Program gets updates too! The last one was around 200 years ago and brought us the theme of Feeling as a possible priority in order to be happy.

Looking at the values of our parents, grand-parents and society in general, we recognise Success and Respect have been the dominant themes shaping the world for thousands of years and are still casting a long shadow in our time. Working long and hard is considered virtuous, making a good impression important, while having fun all day is frowned upon. Somebody making sacrifices is always applauded by society in general, but why?

If you look at how we have changed as a society, especially in the last 100 years, the trend of paying more attention to how we feel has become more important. "Feeling good" is on the way up and about to become an equal member to the other two themes. A third of the population now is putting their foot down and is making "feel good" a priority in their lives. They primarily care about enjoying themselves. They don't care for all the money in the world, if it can't make them feel good. They don't hide their convictions and might think people who suffer in order to be successful are a little bit nuts. In fact, they don't like a difficult and challenging task. They prefer if things go smooth and are a pleasure to do.

Imagine you are a parent with Success and have a child with Feeling, playing video games or having fun all day. Giving such children a lecture they can't have fun all day and that their actions might impact their ability to be successful and secure in life won't work. You can't blackmail them with the same fears a success-driven person might have. You can't lecture them either that everyone in the neighbourhood is already badly talking about them because of what they do. They care little what other people think about them.

Triangle-3 people primarily want to enjoy themselves *now* and rather not invest into something that might offer rewards *later*, especially after long periods of hardship and challenges. You better find the correct thing for that child in order to motivate it in the moment, which can only be something that makes them feel good. Even if they have to do something that is hard and difficult, they need shorter intervals of sacrifices followed by a reward that makes them feel good again. You can't starve them too long from the "feeling good" factor or they drop out. They don't see the point of a prestigious Ivy-League university that sets them up for life, if it's not also fun while doing it. And they are not primarily looking for praise or the image that comes with it. It's important that they always have something in their life that is fun in regular intervals. Then they can also be successful.

Feeling people want to eat their cake right *now*. They don't see the point in investment through prolonged sacrifices to get a bigger cake later. They are so fundamentally different from a Triangle-1 or 2. You can see why some people are not compatible. It's things like this that make up the **baantu.com** relationship stars, that allow you to see how easy or challenging a relationship with somebody can be.

For the *mind* side, a Triangle-3 means using your mind for things that are fun or make you feel good. As always, this includes talking and watching, as well as learning and figuring things out. Many people with this quality are funny themselves or have a little smile on their faces when they talk. They have little time for boring people and boring things, even if they offer great rewards. I guess not many of them are able to study law, although there might be a few who consider this fun. Generally, you see that Triangle-3's react stronger to their change of emotions. They can hide it less. They are not the best "actors".

People with the Triangle-3 can easily blow a fuse despite their initial friendly appearance. If you get in the way of making them feel good, they let off steam and can get angry. "Feeling good" might sound rather pleasant, but it can have a "bad" side (like all others), too. Don't forget Success and Respect (what others think) are *not* the most important thing for them so they don't try to control their emotions. They are guided by emotions. As wonderful as they can be when they are in a good mood, as unpleasant they can be when somebody makes them feel terrible. There is no security mechanism in place as with Success or Respect. It's not unusual for a Feeling person to sabotage their career with an outburst at the wrong time. Who says that being honest will always serve you the best?

Triangle-1's and 2's put up a better show to hide when they're emotionally hurt. They have better control over their emotions for other reasons. They are not ruining their career or their image and shouting at the wrong person or in the wrong place because they feel badly. They don't always wear their emotions on their sleeves. But they can also hide their joy if it might work against them.

Just think about people getting jealous.

If you are a Triangle-3 on the *body* side you want to *do* things in life and meet people that make you feel good. Triangle-3's are the great pleasure seekers in life. Some of them don't see a big career as the most important thing in life, especially when it can't be fun. They also don't watch their waistline all the time and don't always see the point in starving themselves to be successful, look good or admired by others. I'm not saying that all of them are obese, but you will find more Triangle-3's caring less about their appearance when eating something that makes them feel good. They want to enjoy themselves. They want a good quality of life instead of a long struggle. They definitely don't want to meet people or go to places that make them feel bad or are bland and boring. They don't want to do a sport that is unpleasant, difficult and hurts. In a nutshell, they want to avoid suffering as much as possible. Some might even call them over-sensitive (not to be confused with insecure). You have to understand *feeling good* is the centre piece of their life. Pain is the enemy and has no place, if it can be avoided.

Having said that, there are many additional factors we get to hear later that can have a further influence on what you do. The Triangles are only the first chapter about the influences of the Program, shaping who you are. None of these themes are black and white. It's, of course, possible that a Feeling person wants to be successful, but through the influence of the Program, they are fighting an uphill battle and it's much harder for them than a Success person. I personally wouldn't limit myself to any kind of activity, but I understand that some things come easier for me than others, especially when I compare myself with other people. This is really what it's all about: To understand we are all different, that we are not the same. Just because you are different, doesn't mean something is wrong with you.

THE PEOPLE YOU LIKE

In the Graph, there is a row that says "you" and another underneath labelled "others". Both have Triangles, Hexagons and Circles, but possibly different numbers.

We've already learned from the two Triangles how the Program influences us. It shows the quality largely responsible for our mood, what makes us happy or miserable.

When you look at the Triangle in the "others" section, it reveals what kind of people you prefer as company, the kind of people you are attracted to. But you could also interpret it as what qualities you tolerate in other people. All the qualities you learned about in the previous chapter apply here. Now it's not about *your* qualities but these of *other* people. You might be someone whose priority in life is Success, but maybe you don't want people around you whose mood is connected to Success and talk about nothing else all day. Maybe you prefer somebody who is *funny* (Feeling) around you, whose primary goal is not only to get ahead in life. If you have a Triangle-3 in "others", it means the Program influences you through others so that Feeling becomes a part of your life. There is no rational explanation. We don't know "why" we are attracted to people with these qualities. It is all for the benefit of the universe, that living organism we know nothing about. "Others" is a mechanism to form patterns in life. The Program arranges people (and all life) in patterns. It says next to someone like you must be very specific people, and they again have very specific people next to them. If we go back to our comparison of the cells in our own body, we can see how the cells are grouped in very distinctive patterns.

It's an incorrect assumption to say we prefer people who are like us. Some do, others not. BaanTu can get to the bottom of it and tell you exactly what you are looking for in others. But not only that. You can also look whether people you know are looking for the qualities *you* have.

An important aspect you shouldn't ignore here is that the people you surround yourself with have a substantial influence on your life.

All our lives are determined by two things: Our own qualities and the environment we are in. Our environment (the people around us) shape and influence us equally as our own traits we had already possessed when we were born.

Imagine you are a Feeling (fun) person. Your life will take a much different turn if you also prefer to have Feeling people around you, like yourself, compared with Feeling people who like Success people around them.

So the traits you see in "others", in your own Graph,

become a little bit your own, because these people (and their themes) are more present in your life.

People who have *neither* your own theme nor the one shown in "others" are the ones you have little interest in. It's a theme you don't understand and you are not looking for. These people can start to annoy you sooner than others.

MIND

Looking at my own data, I'm a Feeling mind (Triangle-3), but like people with a Success mind (Triangle-1). That means I appreciate people who prioritise Success over Feeling or Respect when using their minds. I like people who are disciplined and can work hard to achieve something in life. I'm less keen on people like myself, who only want to feel good all day and quit when things become unpleasant, although I have sympathy for them (compatibility).

The influence of success-driven people around me,

rubs off on me. It becomes a part of my life and even who I am. I might make a greater effort to work hard, through their influence on me.

When you look at the two Triangles in the illustration, you also see that Triangle-2 (Respect) is not there. Not in "you" and not in "others" (not in myself and the people I prefer). So I don't have much time for people (nor do I "get" them) who are obsessed with Respect. I don't care at all what people think about me and I don't particularly want people around me who always worry what other people think about them. It's just not part of my life.

Always look for the number(s) that are not there. This is what you like less or understand less. It's the theme(s) you have issues with when they become too dominant.

Now go again and look at the people you know. You can already make an analysis at that level. Maybe take a little break from the book and practise a bit at **baantu.com**. Ask the people you know for their birth time, or look at some of the celebrities you know a little bit better. Maybe you've seen a documentary about them or interviews with them.

We only covered the Triangles so far, but it's fascinating how much you already know about a person just by looking at what their priorities in life are. But Triangles are not always the most obvious thing when you meet a person. They can appear to be buried under other things.

It takes time to see it. What you usually see first are the things we come to later in the book (for example the Circles and active Pressure Centres in the Graph). But for the people themselves, it's the Triangle that's the centre of their life, because it determines their happiness. The Pressure Centres, despite the fact they are responsible for our actions, don't control our mood. They only motivate us to do things. They give us focus. They provide you with energy for certain activities.

CONFIDENCE

The Hexagon is the second part of our senses and your way of measuring well-being. We already know from the Triangle which one of the three available themes we prioritise, because they are the key for our happiness. But the Hexagon provides us with an additional quality. It shows how resilient we are when things go wrong. It shows us how long we need to heal. Of course, if you are less resilient, you are more sensitive, more shy and less confident. In a word, you are more easily hurt. You tend to hold a grudge longer, relatively speaking, compared with the other two.

1 – Low (Pessimist)
2 – Medium (Realist)
3 – High (Optimist)

Don't fall into the trap of thinking one of these three themes is better than the other. For you, best is what you are. You can't change any of the Hexagons, Triangles or

Circles anyway. If you are a sensitive person, you get hurt more easily, are less resilient, and more fragile. But because of this, you are more aware of any dangers, which is the reason you are more sensitive. It also gives you less confidence. But instead of blindly jumping to the conclusion that low confidence is "bad", you should see the advantages it also offers. To be aware of the things that can go wrong is a very useful trait.

Don't fight who you are. Work with it. Understand why you are the way you are and what the trigger points are when you react badly and when you react positively. I'm not telling you to avoid or change anything. You can do whatever you like, but now you can see things with a greater awareness. You don't blindly stumble around in a dark room. It's important to see what makes you different from others. We are not all meant to be the same.

What happens when somebody is more sensitive and gets more easily hurt is they are going to shield themselves more from "surprises". They are less available. They want to control who, or what, has access to them. On the body side, they don't allow people easy access who create problems connected to the body. That way they get less hurt. Somebody with a higher resilience doesn't hide. On the mind side, it's the openness for anything mind related. Somebody with a low resilience makes sure they can't be challenged, while the high resilience mind is less threatened by other people's opinion.

PESSIMIST

The Hexagon-1 has the lowest resilience and confidence levels relative to the other two Hexagons. These people are easily hurt, but they are also more sensitive. They know things can always go wrong, which makes them insecure beings. They don't easily trust anyone or anything. Because of this, they start building walls around them so people can't hurt them. They are very private people. They are less "available". The Hexagon tells us how near you let others come to you. If you have a Hexagon-1 body, you're probably uncomfortable with strangers hugging and kissing you.

It's important you don't see the Pessimist as a problem or something you want to run away from. If this is your Hexagon, forget everything people told you about it. Nobody is a "good", "bad", or "handicapped" person. Nobody has more disadvantages or advantages than others. We are all the exact person that the universe wants us to be. I don't care what other people out there "think" I should be. I'm not their slave.

As I already said many times before, every trait we identify in BaanTu has "good" and "bad" sides. They are all lived out differently by all of us, but more than that: The same thing that annoys one person can be a delight for another.

If somebody has a lower resilience level, they have a "thinner" skin. They are not as tough. I realize it sounds like they feel pain more strongly, but that's actually not correct. What happens is they need more time to get over it. They need longer to recover. They don't forget what happened as easily. A Hexagon-3 gets over pain the quickest, whereas the Hexagon-1 gets over it the slowest. If you are more sensitive, you also treat other people differently than the other Hexagons because of this. You have to look whether you have this on the mind or the body side, or both. If you have a Hexagon-1 on the mind side, you get easily hurt by things that are connected to things you are using your mind for, which includes speaking. It means you have less confidence in your mental abilities, and that you have less confidence in your speaking abilities when you are under attack. This has absolutely nothing to do with your actual intelligence or your mentality. You are just more aware about risks and what can go wrong. It's also a reason you might avoid certain situations altogether.

If you have a Hexagon-1 on the body side, you get easily hurt by anything you use your body for or connected to your physical body in general. So if somebody makes fun about your body, you won't forget that for a very long time.

Hexagon-1 people can occasionally hold a grudge forever. For some Hexagon-1's, there can be events in life that are truly traumatic from which they might never recover from. Telling them "to be more confident" is possibly one of the worst pieces of advice you can give. They can't be more confident. All you do is sway them to ignore dangers and then they get hurt even more. It's okay for them to protect themselves by not letting everyone near them, to not be dragged into all kinds of things they're not comfortable with. In the event they are heavily traumatised, therapy can help. But if they want to hide, let them hide. This doesn't mean they'll never come out of hiding. It only means they want to be in control with who they let close, who they allow access to themselves. They want to "screen" people, especially potential trouble makers, before they let them near. They are not as open as a Hexagon-3. If they reach a level of unbearable paranoia, the best approach is to make them feel prepared and protected.

When someone gets hurt, it's not just about physical bruises (having an accident) but also emotional ones – for example, when somebody is rejecting you. Somebody might have a high resiliency on the mind, but a low one on the body. This means they are not easily hurt by things they are using their minds for. Maybe they said the wrong thing and got into trouble, or somebody told them that they are dumb. It wouldn't affect them as much. But having a Hexagon-1 on the body side means they are very sensitive and easily hurt by anything that is connected to their bodies, their physical actions, or the material plane. It would make such a person act very conservatively (body), but still think and speak boldly (mind).

It's important to also look at the Triangle to understand what your resilience is related to. The Hexagons are *always* connected to the Triangles. They work as a pair. If you have Success in the Triangle, the Hexagon-1 means you might tend to be a sore loser. If you have Respect, you are easily hurt when people think poorly of you or hold you in low esteem or disrespect you. What the Hexagon-1 therefore does is try to ensure such people don't get close to them. It's doesn't give people easy access, but most of all only a selected few will be allowed.

Whenever you see a Hexagon-1, "fear" is a big part of that person's life. Don't see this as a problem but an incentive to be perfectly prepared. If you have a Hexagon-1, then fear is something very important in your life.

A Hexagon-1 will always worry about things. That's who they are. If it's the mind, they will worry about what they say. When it's the body, they will worry about what they do. Of course, the same goes for what other people say and do to them.

Later, we will look at a few interesting examples, but it's not uncommon to see some people suffering from depression or alcohol-drug problems, because they are thrown into situations they are not equipped to handle. Famous artists in the public eye can especially suffer terribly with a "thin" skin. They then might resort to drugs and alcohol to deal with their discomfort and fears.

At the same time, some of the greatest poets, songwriters, and singers have great sensitivity and gifts in which to share their suffering and pain in beautiful ways. You can see why we like their art so much, but you can also see how fame can easily destroy them – that sometimes they are not tough enough for the business.

What I don't want to imply is that Hexagon-1 people are more at risk to become an alcoholic or to take drugs. They are not. But you can see the reason why some of them do it. Not everyone that drinks and takes drugs has a problem. Some actually do it for fun and become addicted. For the Hexagon-1, it's probably connected to some kind of trauma related to the Triangle, but even a Hexagon-3 can get hurt. Nobody is invincible. The Hexagon and Triangle always reveal what hurts people the most and it's often the cause for substance abuse. Some feel depressed and carry their hurt inwards, others lash out at others. We all have our own ways of dealing with it. But all three Hexagon groups have a breaking point. The Hexagon-3 only recovers more quickly. It forgets easier.

Some Hexagon-1 people, especially if they have it on both sides, might have trouble coping with the world. This largely depends, of course, on their specific life trajectory and circumstances.

Again, it's a mistake to think one can make them more resilient. The only way that works is to give them a tool to feel more secure by avoiding some of the dangers and triggers. Counselling and therapy might help remove some of the deep traumas, but it can be hard, requiring enormous discipline and dedication. Once a Hexagon-1 is traumatised, it stays with them for a long time. I'm sure there are ways to help them, but my point is: It's not helpful to try to make them into something they can never be. If someone is made sensitive by the Program, they will always be.

The best solution is to remove them from an environment that is unhealthy for them and help them to get over past traumatic events.

Double Hexagon-1's can be quite a challenge for the people around them, who feel like they constantly have to walk on eggshells. No matter what they do, it can feel like they always say or do the wrong thing to the Hexagon-1.

Because many of them start building walls around them or have trust issues, it's not rare for them to end up alone for big parts of their lives. Usually, it's what they want, so you don't always have to feel sorry for them.

If somebody is sensitive, they are also more likely to treat others with more sensitivity. When you have it on the mind, you are more sensitive with what you say to others and when you are sensitive on the body, you might physically treat others with more sensitivity.

Hexagon-1 people have the strongest sense of shame, whereas the Hexagon-3 almost feels no shame at all. If it's on the mind, it's about what you say, if it's on the body side, it's about what you do and how you present your body.

Another interesting observation is that a Hexagon-1 prefers familiar things and people. Of course, a familiar object or person comes with less risk and that's what the Hexagon-1 prefers. It prefers the familiar over the unfamiliar. I've seen quite a few Hexagon-1 people who love old movies, whereas this is not something I'm particularly fond of as a Hexagon-3 mind. I'm more adventurous and have broader interests. I always love to see new things. My mind loves surprises. A Hexagon-3 body would always love to meet new people, whereas a Hexagon-1 probably prefers to deal with the people it knows well. "Familiarity" is important for Hexagon-1's. If they found something that works for them, they might do it for the rest of their lives.

I'm a Hexagon-1 on the body and I hate eating things I don't know. But I'm more than happy to eat the few things I do know and like for the rest of my life. I don't need a great variety.

You can see that whatever I use my mind for, I like

surprises and new things (I'm not afraid of things I don't know), whereas anything I use my body for or affects my body, I prefer a routine that has proven to work.

REALIST

Here we have someone who is much better equipped to deal with failure or attacks from other people than the Hexagon-1. This person is not so easily traumatised. They are tougher, but also know their limits. They can deal with failure and criticism with much more grace and ease than the 1, but they are by no means indestructible. There are certain jobs that are not for them. But because they are less afraid, they are also more accessible than the 1. They don't hide so much. They are not afraid to be on social media, which can often make the 1 very uncomfortable.

They are neither a Pessimist like the 1 nor an Optimist like the 3. They are in the middle and what I call a Realist. They have a realistic outlook at life. They don't worry all the time, but are no dreamers, totally unaware of the risks. They are aware of risks and dangers, but not paralysed by them. They are confident, but not over-confident. They don't run away from everything, but are also not trying everything. They are selective, almost calculating, in what they say and who they want to involve themselves with and what not.

Again, "realistic" probably sounds like a "good" compromise and a "good" Hexagon, but it's not better or worse then the other two. You can't change your resilience. You can't toughen up when you are sensitive. What we do with BaanTu is not change who you are, but make you aware of your nature so you can have a better understanding about why you react to certain situations in a certain way – why you are different from other people you know. If you try to change who you are, it can be frustrating and only exacerbate problems. Instead, it's better to find ways to work with who you are.

Your level of confidence and the time you need to heal are traits you can't change. All you can do if you are a Hexagon-1 is remove the dangers from your life by shielding yourself from harm, but that doesn't make you more confident. It removes a threat as much as possible in order to manage fear. And that's all that matters. The Hexagon-2 is the most realistic theme. These people are usually not paranoid, and yet they don't see life through rose-coloured glasses either. They seem to make reasonable decisions.

As before, when you have this theme on the mind side, you can deal with a realistic level of criticism or failure for anything connected to your mental abilities.

You have a medium confidence level as a speaker and are realistic about how capable you are with your ideas and intelligence. You don't run away when things get ugly, but you also probably don't want to deal with a "chaotic house on fire". You might be more open to allow certain people to challenge you. You don't silence every critic like the 1 might. You are more open to what other people have to say, but only to a certain degree. There is a limit to how much you can take before feeling seriously hurt or the need to run away when things get ugly.

The same applies for the body side. You can deal well with rejection connected to your body to a certain point, which makes you more resilient than the 1 and less paranoid when you deal with other people. You are also more confident in your own body and appearance as the 1, but at the same time, you don't think you are perfect as the Hexagon-3 might. You are quite aware of flaws and limitations.

Don't forget the Hexagon primarily determines how much access that you allow others to have to you. A low resilience level needs to be in total control of who can be allowed through the door. They don't trust anyone or anything. They need the most protection. The 2 needs to have less control, but not unrestricted access. It can deal with certain surprises, but not everything. The 3 doesn't worry at all and doesn't "screen" people. It's open to anyone, and up for anything.

You can see why the 2 is occasionally seen as a snob, because they only let a certain kind of person near, while rejecting others. The 1 rejects almost everything unfamiliar or risky. It has a very narrow door, while the 3 has no door at all. It can deal with anything. Hexagon-2's, on the other hand, are selective. They are available to very specific things and people. There is a calculating quality to the Hexagon-2. Some might call it "risk assessment", others "snobby behaviour". While the 1 says "no" to most unfamiliar things and the 3 "yes" to almost anything (in order to find out how it is or what it is), the 2 probably gives you a "maybe, depending on the circumstances".

OPTIMIST

Here we come to the most confident group of all. They almost don't know what fear is. They are not easily intimidated. Of course, what might be an advantage in certain situations might also get you "killed" in others. They live in total denial of some of the dangers. You might call them dreamers. Again, like the other hexagons, this has nothing to do with a superior intelligence or abilities. But if any can make dreams come true, it's them, because they are not afraid to lose. They aim high in life.

Do you feel you are equipped to deal with all kinds of situations and people? Or do you prefer to narrow it down to something very specific, where you have better control in what you have to deal with? The Hexagon-3 feels it's equipped to deal with anything life is throwing at them (which doesn't mean it is). Of course, you must see if you have this on the body or mind side. The Hexagon-2 would see the 1 and 3 as somewhat unrealistic.

A Hexagon-1 always worries, while the Hexagon-3 almost never worries. They don't think anything could go wrong. This is what makes them such optimists and dreamers. When they get hurt, they recover incredibly quickly. They have this ability to quickly move on from a "bad moment". They get back on their feet more quickly.

Of course, we can have mental "moments" and physical "moments". It's hard for an Hexagon-3 mind to hold a grudge against anyone for a long time. At least not when it comes to using their minds. They don't easily lose their cool and don't run away from a difficult argument that might result in heavy accusations or personal attacks. They don't feel easily threatened. They don't try to silence others. They don't hide. They are available. To understand mind versus body, it's not whether people hurt you with words or actions. It's about what part of you they attack. Do you get attacked for something that you were using your body for? Or did you get attacked for something you were using your mind for? If you have a high resilience on the body (Hexagon-3 body) and somebody makes an awful comment about your body or about something you did using your body, it won't hurt you for long. But if you have a Hexagon-1 mind and somebody makes fun of your "stupid" idea or how you speak, you won't forget this for a very long time.

Of course, nobody likes being attacked, but the Hexagon-3 quickly gets over it compared with the other hexagons. It recovers sooner relative to the others.

What might take a while to become accustomed with is the different combinations between levels of sensitivity on the body and mind sides.

If you take my example, I have the highest resiliency level mind (3), but the most sensitive body (1).

I'm easily hurt when people make fun of my body or criticise what I do. I don't deal well with rejection of my physical abilities or actions and remember it for a long time. This makes me physically extremely shy, but on the mind side I'm the polar opposite. Here, I'm not concerned at all. I never feel defenceless with my mind. I always think I'm able to solve things. I'm never afraid of a heated argument where people criticise my ideas or what I said. I'm not saying it's pleasant in the moment, but I get over it very quickly. I don't freeze when it happens. A heated exchange about things concerning my mind stimulates me. I don't hide from it. But anything connected with my physical abilities, then I'm easily intimidated.

I'm a confident public speaker. It doesn't scare me to be "out there". But what I don't like is if people have unrestricted physical access to me. They can challenge my mind, but I don't let most people physically close. I'm reserved and distant. I don't appreciate people who want to meet me or visit unless I want to see them. I'm a private person. Hexagon-1's are recluses. I don't let a lot of people get close to me. I don't like a lot of physical contact. I prefer a physical distance to most. But a Hexagon-3 mind doesn't have a lot of secrets. It has nothing to hide. Same with the Hexagon-3 body, it has no or little physical shame.

A Hexagon-3 not only tends to be less sensitive when it comes to themselves, but also how they act. A Hexagon-3 mind might say things to others that could easily hurt them without realising it. You could say they have a big mouth. They can be quite rude. A Hexagon-3 body person might physically act with less sensitivity, making others uncomfortable sometimes without realising it and at other times on purpose. If you have a Hexagon-3 and someone else has a Hexagon-1, the risk you might hurt them or they think you are acting insensitively is always bigger. But to see the full picture look at their Hexagon in "others". It tells you what kind of people they tolerate and who they don't. Basically, you understand and have empathy for people like yourself (they have the same numbers as you), but you tolerate and admire people who have the numbers that you have in the "others" row.

Because a Hexagon-3 is less afraid of things going wrong,

they have a tendency to prepare less and like to improvise instead. They just begin with something and then take it from there. A Hexagon-1 would only come fully prepared or not at all. They have a tendency to stay with familiar things and people, which minimises the risk of failure and saves them any tedious preparation work. The Hexagon-2 would only prepare at a reasonable level and rarely over-prepare. It doesn't come unprepared, but it also doesn't prepare for every possible scenario and can improvise to a certain degree. The Hexagon-3 doesn't need any script at all. It is always ready for anything.

But it's not just about how much you prepare, it's also about how much in advance you start with your preparations. The Hexagon-1 would start the earliest, the Hexagon-2 in reasonable time and the Hexagon-3 would usually prepare at the last minute (or not at all). If a task looks too daunting, the Hexagon-1 would not even try, whereas the Hexagon-3 has more of a "let's try and see what happens" approach.

INTERACTION TYPE

The Circle is not connected to the senses. It's not about your mood either, but rather about how we get things done. Like the other symbols, there are three different types of interaction. They are similar to players in a football game (soccer for our American friends). We have people who are attacking, the pushers, the visionaries who initiate. Then we have people who are defensive. They respond to things. They wait for things to come, they respond. But there are also the mid-fielders, the bridge between responding and attacking. They are looking for opportunities. They are, similar to the Hexagon-2, more selective.

1 – Reactor (patient)
2 – Opportunist (calculating)
3 – Initiator (impatient)

What's interesting is that nobody can have the same Interaction Type on both the body and mind side, nobody can have the same number in both Circles. If your mind is an Initiator (Circle-3) you can't be an Initiator with the body. If your body is a Reactor (Circle-1), your mind can't be too.

A Reactor has a wait-and-see approach. It waits for life to come and reveal where the journey goes. It waits for other people to turn up offering possibilities.

The Initiator, on the other hand, wants to be in control of what happens and has expectations. It knows what it wants and goes after it. It hates to be told what to do. It wants to be in control of its destiny.

Reactors are more open to invitations and suggestions. But don't make the mistake to think Reactors can't get far in life. The only difference might be that some of them will say much later in life: "I would have never thought that things would turn out like this!", whereas the Initiator might tell you: "I already knew at the age of 15 what I wanted and went after it!"

An Initiator feels much more in control of its path, but as I've already said, nature doesn't allow people to be an Initiator on both the mind and body sides. There is always one side in your programming that makes you more controlling and another side making you a little more receptive to discover where fate is taking you.

The 2/3 or 3/2 Circle types in general might be pushier than the rest, with the 1/2 or 2/1 the most passive type.

REACTOR

A Circle-1 (Reactor) is much more comfortable reacting rather than attacking or initiating. They are not in the business of upsetting or bothering people. They are very patient and wait for others to turn up instead of going after them. They have a passive approach in life. They don't have their whole life mapped out in advance. They wait and see where life is taking them. They are not constantly pushing the boat. They usually don't want to be the one who gets the ball rolling. They are not Initiators. They don't like to chat people up or provoke them with some kind of idea out of the blue. Instead, they like to be asked. They like to be invited. They have no problem waiting for the right invitation or their turn. But they don't turn up uninvited or invite themselves, like a Circle-3 (Initiator) might do.

Generally, Reactors don't like to bother or upset you, unless you did something to them. They are not attackers, they are responders. They might become aggressive in their defence, but even that depends on their Hexagon (sensitivity).

As always, we have a mental and physical component coming from the two different Bhan Crystals controlling us. When you have a Reactor (Circle-1) mind, you are not in the business of upsetting other people for no reason with what you say. You are not using your mind to Initiate. You are not necessarily trying to convince people with an idea unless they have asked for it or invited you to voice your opinion.

The body Reactor (Circle-1) is the physical counterpart and not too interested in making first contact with others. They'd rather let someone else make the first move and then respond. They try less to control their destiny and instead would rather observe what life is offering them. They make themselves available, but how easy they are to "find" depends on the Hexagon. It can feel like they need an extra invitation before they start doing things with their bodies or doing things affecting their bodies.

To see the potential of a Reactor largely depends on the environment and what that brings out of the person. You will never know what they are capable of doing if you never ask them. This doesn't necessarily mean they don't know what they want. They might, but it's about timing and when to act. This is where they surrender to the flow of life. Passivity doesn't mean a person is not discerning or discriminating. A Reactor is like a well where other people drink from.

OPPORTUNIST

The Opportunist is very adept at turning things around. Similar to the mid-fielder in a football game, they can turn around the direction of the ball. All of a sudden, they switch from a passive role to an active one.

Opportunists have the patience to wait. But compared with the Reactor, they are not waiting for an invitation, but for an opportunity. They are observers, are selective, and calculating. This is similar to the Hexagon-2, but instead of assessing risks, it's about assessing prospects.

Let's look at my own example on the body side. I have a Hexagon-1, combined with a Circle-2.

BODY

YOU

I'm a private person and make it difficult for people to

physically reach me. The door is only open for very few. I'm not comfortable if strangers turn up or get in touch with me. I don't want anybody to "surprise" me. I hate it when people are "forced" upon me by others. I want to be in total control of who has access to me. I prefer some kind of a distance. This is how I control getting hurt, because I have a low resilience (Hexagon-1). It makes me physically shy and also easily worried. I don't blindly trust people or life or my physical abilities.

When we look at the Circle though, I'm not just waiting for invitations, I'm an Opportunist. I like to be in control of my destiny on the material plane to a certain degree. But I hate to bother the "wrong" people. I don't want to waste my time with the wrong things. Once I'm satisfied that I'm presented with an opportunity, I might accept an invitation or even initiate. But many times, I can give the impression of being quite passive, waiting for something, only to surprise people how active, and what a determined driving force, I can become, once the right opportunity, once the thing that "clicks" comes along.

INITIATOR

Here we come to the type of person who wants to be in control. They don't wait for life to hand them the keys. They don't have a lot of patience. Once they know what they want, they try to get it. They go after things. But depending on their confidence (Hexagon), they might have different methods.

An Initiator is always in "attack" mode. They always try to "sell" you something. If they have the Circle-3 on the mind side, they might sell you their vision, plans, or opinions. They are not waiting for an invitation or the right moment. They might interrupt more often relative to the others. They tell people their vision or agenda or thoughts without prompting. Whether anyone really wants to hear it or not is almost not the point. There is always a slight impatience present, up to a varying point of being pushy.

If they have the Circle-3 on the body side, they use their body to initiate, push, and "attack". They are the adventurers. They want to see the world. They get up, pick a place, and set out to go there. They are travellers. They are not waiting for an invitation or opportunity. They want to be in total control of where life takes them. They also make others do things. They chat people up, they knock at their doors. They know what they want and they find a way to get it. But they absolutely hate being told by others what they can or cannot or should do. It's the same with the Circle-3 mind. They don't want to hear from others what they should think or say.

They are not always the best listeners, unless what you say is related to their own agenda. They are too busy initiating and don't want to get distracted from their own path. They have less patience when listening and usually only wait for their opportunity to say their opinion. If the opportunity doesn't come, they hijack the conversation or event anyway.

Even when you look at social media, there are people making statements, people with a vision, and producing content, and then there are people reacting to what goes on there and re-posting it. This is similar to the defenders and strikers in football. A Circle-3 doesn't want to get sucked into responding too much (unless it is connected to whatever they are initiation), because it prevents them from going after their own goals.

People with a Circle-3 can be intense, because they never seem to wait. Of course, anyone "attacking" or putting things out is taking a risk of getting rejected. The Hexagon will determine just how outrageous they get. The Hexagon-1 would tread more lightly, but still initiate and attack. They would probably check for any possible setbacks first or prepare incredibly well. But they would still initiate and not wait for things to come to them. The Hexagon-3 doesn't worry about setbacks. They say what they have to say to *everyone* whenever it pleases them. A double 3 mind (like mine in the illustration below) is the most confident thinker and speaker. They are the most open, but also the most aggressive in an argument if necessary. They don't hide what they think and they interrupt if necessary. They have an idea or vision and don't settle for the "second best" opportunity. They are less interested in anyone else's vision. It's easier to suggest something to a 1 than to a 3. The 3's only want to hear something when it concerns what they are already working on.

MIND

To see the full picture for my data (including the Triangle), my theme for happiness (determining my mood) would be Feeling. So it's important for me to use my mind and say things in order to feel good or have fun. It's less about reaching a goal (Triangle-1) or what others think about me (Triangle-2). At the same time, you can begin to understand how my reaction would be if somebody is boring or makes me feel bad. I'm not the most sensitive person with my mind (Hexagon-3), so I can be quite rude and outspoken. I don't usually hold back with my opinion. Fun (Triangle-3), combined with no fear (Hexagon-3) as well as being an Initiator can make me sarcastic. It's a lot of fun for me, but can hurt others. Sometimes I don't even realise it. And I also do it whenever I want, because I'm an Initiator. I might just interrupt you when you speak, maybe making a silly joke. I'm known for offending people with uninvited criticism. A Hexagon-1 would be easily hurt by people like me, unless they have my numbers in "others", which means they tolerate my behaviour more and for some strange reason even find it attractive. Luckily, to the relief of some, I'm very different on the body side. And so is everyone else with the combination Hexagon-3/Circle-3 mind. They all must be very sensitive when they act with their bodies and must have a Hexagon-1.

On the body side, Circle-3's are adept in physically "going after" people and things. Of course, the most confident people would be the ones with the double 3 Hexagon/Circle combination on the body side. Yet, I repeat: It's not always the most confident ones who yield the best results. Don't fall into the trap that 3's (Hexagon or Circle) are better or more successful in life.

Some people (also depending on what they have in the "others" Hexagon/Circle) might find an overconfident person or someone in constant "attack mode" extremely unpleasant or rude. A Circle-3 body has high expectations on the material plane. They know what they want to do with their bodies and they don't wait for an invitation. They go after places *and* people. Many of them travel a lot. Some are successful Formula 1 drivers. As always, there are many examples.

What they all have in common is that they want to be in control and set the pace. Depending on which side the Circle-3 is, they set the pace and direction for what they think or speak, or what they physically do. Both are the Great Seducers. They both have a plan. And they need to be in charge. Most of all, they are very insistent. How much they listen or pay attention to others also depends very much on the Pressure Centres, which we will get to see later in the book.

It is not possible for any of us to have a Circle-3 on the body *and* mind side. The Program does not permit that combination or sequence. I guess that might be a little bit too much! Nobody can have any Circle number on both sides. In my observations, I've found people who have the Circle-2 on the mind side with a Circle-3 on the body to be incredibly successful at seducing others. Some have a lot of affairs. Others are sales people in anything from insurance policies to properties to cars. They go after you with both mind *and* body. They are a physical Initiator as well as a mental Opportunist. There are many examples in how this quality can be lived out.

The Circle-3 mind with Circle-2 body combination is different. They are less about opening physical doors, but adventurers in the mental realm, with ideas and opinions.

The Circle-3 mind will always say things and speak up when they feel like it. You might also say that they complain a lot. It's their Hexagon that will determine how rude and aggressive they can be, while doing that.

Circle-3 bodies can always bother people with what they do and Circle-3 minds do this with their opinions and ideas.

What's fascinating is the distinct pattern of these sequences. There isn't an unlimited array of combinations, contrary to assumptions. As I already hinted earlier, every 3/2 (mind/body), the mental Initiator/physical Opportunist, must have a confident (Hexagon-3) mind and an insecure (Hexagon-1) body. The 2/3 (mind/body) though doesn't have that restriction. Only the 3/2 (mind/body) does. Statistically, the 3/2 is also much rarer. Only 2.6% of people have a 3/2. But 34% have a 2/3. A 3/2 only has a sequence that includes a double 3 on the mind (Hexagon and Circle), so they need to be dreamers and confident when they speak, but then they also must have

88

a Hexagon-1 on the body side, making them pessimistic on the physical, material plane, despite their optimistic minds. They don't trust people. They know things can always go wrong. They are private. It's this, which can turn them into control freaks, but also gives them a greater sensitivity when they act. Check out again my own data.

With **baantu.com,** you can search and browse others based on these combinations. Go to the help section to find out how you can search for people with certain numbers in their Triangles, Hexagons, and Circles.

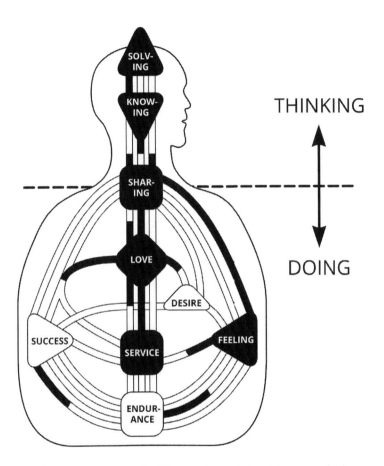

In the same way as the Triangle and the Hexagon belong together (they both measure), we also have a "partner" for the Circles and that's the Pressure Centres. Here, it's about acting, not measuring. We have nine Pressure

Centres and these centres occur in pairs.

As discussed in the earlier chapter, the Circle reveals if a person likes to initiate or would instead prefer to wait for the right opportunity or invitation. But what is it that they are actually going to do? What kind of activity? The information in the rather complex drawing within the human shape of the Graph shows *Channels* connecting the nine *Pressure Centres*. They show us what somebody wants to do. They show us their motivation for certain things, they show their focus.

You must understand Pressure Centres and Channels are not reflecting the only activity that you can do. We are not limited like that. We are autonomous beings. In principle, we can do whatever we want, but the Program has ways of interfering. What the Channels and Pressure Centres show are conditions that the Program insists upon. For example, if you see "Love" active, it insists that you do something that you love or you are with people that you love. When you have "Solving", the Program insists that you question and solve things (using your mind). You can do whatever you like, unless you take the themes of the active Channels and Centres on board.

There are two ways how the Program gets you to follow this. First, you feel a motivation towards these themes. On the other hand, if you do something that violates them, the Program "pulls the plug" and you run out of energy.

Don't make the mistake in assuming, for instance, that if somebody doesn't have "Solving" active they can't solve things. Of course they can, but they don't have to. The Program isn't insisting on it. But somebody with Solving defined is under constant pressure to do just that. As we will see later, these Channels also have very specific themes, usually for a larger purpose involving the community or collective. They are not personal. In essence, the Program gives you a job that you have to do. It's like going to work. But when you come home, you are free to do whatever you want in your spare time.

The biggest difference between the three symbols (Triangle, Hexagon, Circle) and the Channels and Pressure Centres is that the latter always change over time either through the planets or the people you meet. The three symbols, on the other hand, stay the same throughout your life. First though, let's try to understand what a Channel is.

Sometimes there is only half of a Channel. A full Channel is formed out of two *Gates*, each of them coming out of a Pressure Centre. These Gates become activated by the position of the planets in our solar system. Every planet activates a certain Gate depending on its position in the sky. Some of these activated Gates also form a Channel. Sometimes they don't though, in which there will only be half a Channel. If you want to see what planet activates what Gate, press the Wheel button on **baantu.com**. When you hover with the mouse over any planet in the wheel, the corresponding Gate that it activates in the Graph will be highlighted. This is easier to understand once you go there and try it for yourself.

The Channels and Gates in the drawing at the beginning of this chapter are the ones I always have active in my life. They are calculated based on my exact birth time. But we also have additional Channels and Gates that get activated through the *current* position of the same planets, which we don't see in this drawing. Because the planets move at different speeds, parts of our Graph also change with it accordingly. This book will later get into this in more detail. In the BaanTu software, these additional Channels and Gates will be highlighted with the help of the *Transit* button or the *Period* buttons (48 hours, week, month, or half year).

The nine Pressure Centres and Channels symbolise the motivation a person has to do certain tasks or activities. Again, the focus is on the "doing". What might be confusing at first is, say, Success in the Triangle compared with Success defined in the Pressure Centre. But you must understand that what you actually do in your life is primarily the result of an active Channel, as it regulates your energy flow. The Triangle then judges the experience from the viewpoint of the Triangle theme and sets your mood. Depending on the resulting mood, you will alter how you do things, or in extreme cases stop altogether and look for something else that fits what the currently active Channels want.

Not only do the active Channels motivate you towards a specific type of activity, they also determine what particular activity you are given energy for. You can view the Channels and Pressure Centres as "energy regulators". They divide up the available energy you possess for certain activities. What they also do is cut your energy supply for activities that don't match the requirements seen by the activations. Let's say that you have Feeling active in the Graph. The moment you do things that don't make you or others feel good, you will run out of energy, which of course, also results in a low motivation. Running out of energy is not the same as being in a bad mood.

If you see a hanging Gate, as in my Graph with the Gate hanging to the left of *Love*, it isn't doing anything. It's not felt. It's not active. It would need another Gate reaching from the other side to activate this Channel. Only Channels are functional and motivating. A Gate is only a mere possibility. It is reaching out to something.

Here comes the interesting thing: Not only can a Transit (the current position of the planets) make a new connection with a Gate, other people's hanging Gates can do the same thing. If you meet somebody who makes a connection with one of your hanging Gates, you both feel an increased motivation to do something together. This only works when you both have a hanging Gate and not the full Channel. Before we get into all the details of this, let's talk about what the various Pressure Centres and Channels connecting them actually mean.

Although looking at the active Centres of a person gives you a solid first impression, a better way to begin interpreting a Graph is by looking at the Channels that connect them. Every active Channel has a Pressure Centre on each end, which is what I meant earlier when I said that they come in pairs. For example, if Love is defined, there must be something else connected to it. One Centre alone can't occur. In my case (illustration at the top), Love is connected with Sharing. An example of interpreting this would be: "Sharing with others what you love."

Or "Sharing something with the people you love" or "Sharing something that people love."

In the earlier chapters dealing with the Triangles, Hexagons, and Circles, there is a set of these symbols to the left of the head in the Graph for the body (doing), and another to the right of the Graph for the mind (thinking).

With the nine Pressure Centres, there is also a mind/body division, with a horizontal dividing line through the Sharing Centre. All Gates and Channels above the line are mental activities, everything below are physical activities. The interpretations of body and mind are similar to the earlier chapters. When you think about the influence of the always-moving planets and the constant influx of people coming in and out of your life, this is a complex and dynamic construct. BaanTu (the web site) can help you see it clearer by breaking down some of the aspects into themes like *creativity, community, success,* and so forth. You can see which person activates certain themes of motivation. Let's stay with your own data for the moment.

You can always do more than the Channels and Pressure Centres show. They are not exclusive. They are more of a reminder. It's something you *must* do. Remember, we are autonomous beings. We can make our own decisions. But we are also influenced by the Program. We can do things we want, but also, there are things we must do.

The Graph only shows us what the Program insists on getting done. We are always free to do anything else whenever we want as long as we are able to. But if we have a strong motivation to do certain things (the Program reminding us what it needs you to do), there might not be enough time to do other things or they might seem less important to us. There is always the possibility to do *more* than what the Graph shows, on the condition that we don't lose sight of the bigger goal of what the Program wants from us. The Program doesn't give us all the details. It's up to us to work most of these things out through our own intelligence and life experience.

SOLVING

This Centre is all about figuring out things. It can only appear together with Knowing (which we'll discuss in the next chapter), because all of its Channels connect with Knowing. This is an example of Pressure Centres as a pair. When you *solve* something, you also *know* something.

What you should understand is that when somebody has Solving *not* defined, it's not an indication of a person's intelligence. This simply means the Program puts no consistent pressure on a person to solve. While you theoretically can do anything you want in addition to what the Program wants (we are autonomous), you probably will spend the majority of your time with the themes (Centres and Channels) that are defined.

There are three different kinds of pressures for Solving, explaining the three Channels going to Knowing. We will discuss these subtleties in the Circuits chapter, but for the moment you must understand that all three of them have a value for something larger than yourself. Examples would be the community or the collective. There is pressure to solve something to improve the life of others. It's not just for your own enjoyment.

Anyone (even people with no definition in this

Centre) can still solve things, but more importantly, they can solve things that might have no value for others.

70% of the people have no permanently defined Solving Centre and therefore little desire or time to figure things out. That tells you a lot about our world and why people are so easily manipulated. They'd rather let other people solve things.

KNOWING

When you know something, it doesn't necessarily mean you've figured out what you know *yourself*. You might have "borrowed" knowledge from somebody else. This Centre is available for two kinds of *Knowing*: Knowing that comes from solving something yourself, or knowing (knowledge) that is shared with others. It can either be connected to the Solving Centre above or the Sharing Centre below. When you have Knowing defined, it means there is pressure or an increased motivation felt (the Program insists) to share something of value with others, or to understand (solve) something that has a value for others. Sharing can also mean to listen.

Not every intellectual sees the need to understand what they know when they trust their sources. They might stuff their head full with knowledge and quote things all day long without actually verifying or understanding anything. Memorising (knowing) is not the same as understanding (solving). Both have their own advantages. People borrowing knowledge from others without figuring out for themselves can have quicker results. Of course, if Solving is not defined, there is also greater vulnerability for misinformation and mistakes.

I myself have Solving and Knowing defined in my Graph (page 91), which means if someone gives me information, I always feel the need to verify it before using or memorizing it. I have a work-colleague who doesn't have Solving permanently defined and he sometimes gets annoyed with me, because every time he finds a method for how to solve a problem with a computer code, he copy/pastes it and is done, while I can't accept this. I then spend quite a bit of time trying to understand what the code does and how it works before I use it.

Things like this, by the way, are part of the "compatibility" calculation on the relationship page at **baantu.com**. It tells you how patient (or not) other people are with you.

When you see words like Knowing in BaanTu, you have to look at them in the broadest possible way. It's not just about learning something, like studying at school. Basically, it means you like to watch and that you are curious. Many people who have Knowing are not intellectuals by any stretch of the imagination, but very curious people. Some might just want to know what everyone else is doing or they are heavy gossipers or they always ask questions. They want to be informed. With some of these people, you could feel like you're being constantly interrogated. As I said, there are many paths to Knowledge.

SHARING

This Centre is unique as it can have connections to the mind as well as to the body. It motivates you to *share* what you know (mind) or share something that's connected to the material plane (body). You could also call it *mental* and *physical* sharing.

There are many forms of sharing. Firstly, there can be a verbal sharing. This form of sharing can come out of the mind by sharing something you know, or out of a physical activity or sensation. But you can share in more ways than with words. For example, you can share by taking people along with you on an experience or your wealth or what you physically possess. Or sharing things with other people to make them physically feel good.

Sharing is a two-way street. It's not only about giving, but also about listening and receiving. It's about doing things together. If you have Sharing and Knowing defined, you either find out something (knowing) through somebody else who is sharing with you, or you tell somebody something you know.

When you have Sharing defined, it simply means that the Program puts pressure on you to share with others, to spend time with them. If you want to get an idea of the purpose of your spent time together, then look at the other end of the Channel and its connected Centre.

Similar to the other Centres, if Sharing isn't defined, it doesn't mean this person can never share. Not at all. Instead, it means the Program doesn't put pressure on them – it doesn't insist. They might share or might not, but they don't *have* to. For people who have a Centre defined, it's no longer a choice they can make. They feel a strong urge that is hard to resist. So the chances of it happening increase a lot.

Sometimes Sharing can also be related to generosity, but you have to be very careful with such oversimplified judgments. These are just examples and we all live these Pressure Centres out in different ways. Don't fall into the trap of attaching moral prejudices to the Centres. Every Centre can be lived out "bad" and "good". It really depends on the individual and how life has formed them over time and through their environment.

For example, it's too easy to think somebody with Success sells their granny to get what they want and that Feeling is always nice. This is really not how it works. Everything here can be expressed "good" and "bad", different people will live things out differently. In some cases it might annoy some, in others not at all or be rather pleasant. But if you don't have a Centre yourself and the theme is also not in your Triangles, you generally have less understanding for it. You are less compatible with such a person.

LOVE

Don't worry if you don't have this Centre defined. It doesn't mean you carry less love, that you are less loved by others or a less loving person.

Love is a place. It's where you belong. It's an influence of the Program to position you relative to other people and things. But love can also change.

Because this Centre is below Sharing, it is related to physical activities and the material plane. The material plane includes, of course, other people. What *Love* means in the context of the Graph is that you either feel a strong desire to do what you love or you want to focus on people you love instead of people you don't really care about or don't like. It also means that you do something that other people love.

Love is not a choice made by logic. It's felt as an attraction that we didn't choose. It's a place or person where we feel at home. It's a yearning within us. We are capable to suffer for love. We are able to make great sacrifices for love, no matter if it's for a person or the things we love. And many of us know that love comes with no guarantee to feel good.

When you see a person where Love is not defined, it means they are less restricted in their activities or choice of people. They don't have to "love" everything they do or every person that they are with. They usually have a larger circle of friends, but in truth some of them are probably more loose acquaintances and not close friends. An undefined Love Centre makes it possible to spend time with people and things that you like less or that you are indifferent about. You also have a much higher tolerance.

Let me give you an example: Let's say that in order to be more successful you have to meet someone that you can't stand. Or maybe you have to do something that you don't love to earn more money. This would be a lot easier for someone with an undefined Love Centre compared with someone who has it defined. If you have Love defined, it's increasingly difficult to be with people you don't like, no matter what other advantages a contact with these people could offer. People with undefined Love are comfortable doing a wider range of activities, whereas the defined ones would have a lower tolerance towards things and people they don't love.

Do you understand now what I meant when I said that every aspect in BaanTu has a "good" and a "bad" side? Everything has advantages and disadvantages. What matters is to see who you are instead of fighting yourself due to incorrect ideas about yourself that may have been planted in your head by others. When the mind wants to see something, it has this incredible power to make you believe something is there which isn't.

DESIRE

Anybody with this Centre defined can be incredibly stubborn. All the Channels and Centres represent the Pressure of the Program, and more accurately, your motivations for certain activities. It's a channelling of your energy towards certain kinds of activities.

This Centre is best understood if you negate it. This, by the way, works well for many things in BaanTu. When you look at something, don't just think what it is, also think what it isn't. To focus on your desire is to focus on what you want, what you wish for. But it also means you don't get sidetracked by things you *don't* want to do. You can sidetrack yourself, but often we get sidetracked by things other people want from us. I'm not saying this is bad. Some people are meant to get more sidetracked than others.

People with a defined Desire Centre are really good at saying "no". They can appear incredibly stubborn. No matter how you try to convince them, they remain steadfast and keep saying "no" if they don't want to do something. A defined Desire Centre helps you to stay on track with things that matter to yourself – staying true to your convictions.

65% of the population do not have this Centre permanently defined, which means they often get side tracked with unimportant things that don't matter to them. They do things, despite the fact they know that they shouldn't do them. This Centre has the second highest occurrence of undefined Centres in the population, with Solving taking the top spot. You could also say people with undefined Desire lack the determination to say "no" to things they don't want to do. If you are one of them, don't feel bad. It's not your fault and it makes no difference in terms of your happiness. You are occasionally meant to do things you don't want to do.

For some of us, the way to happiness is by saying "no" to things we don't want to do, while others have a tendency to get sidetracked, because the Program doesn't care if they get sidetracked. They are more open to getting pulled away from what they want, but it doesn't mean they are less happy. Only when people have Desire defined, do we see an intervention of the Program, where it insists that someone stays with what they want.

SERVICE

When this Centre becomes activated, you feel motivated to pay attention to what other people want. Service means "to be of service" in the context of the Graph. The focus is more on other people and less on yourself. This doesn't mean you are necessarily a slave to others. Although you might be actually doing something for somebody else, other examples of this might be to be aware of what other people want. It makes whatever you do more connected to the desires and wishes of others – some might say more commercial.

Of course as always, you have a Centre on the other end of the Channel too, so you could end up with a combination of *Service* and *Love*. In this case you feel pressure to focus on things other people want, but also things that *you* love. At the same time it could mean what other people need and love. You see how the Program narrows down the choices available to you by influencing your motivation? The same Pressure Centre combination could also mean doing things people want, but only for the people you actually care about.

The more Centres you have activated, the more

someone is motivated or under pressure, but at the same time the spectrum of available choices becomes narrower, because there are conditions attached with every Centre.

70% of the population have the Service Centre permanently defined, which means that most of the time they are busy doing things for other people. They represent the builders and commercial work-force of the world.

In so many ways the Service Centre is almost an opposite of the Desire Centre. You could say that Desire is about what *you* want, while Service is about what *others* want. You might wonder what happens when you have both activated in a person. It's not a problem, contrary to what you might initially think. You are still able to find an activity that is something that other people want, but also something that you want to do. These themes are not mutual exclusive.

SUCCESS

This is the second time we meet the theme of Success. The difference is that here you are motivated to *act* to be successful. It's not about measuring and judging.

It's not the Triangles that primarily control your activities, it's the Channels that do that. And whatever happens along these activities is measured by the Triangle and Hexagon and then responsible for the pain and pleasure that you experience – in a nutshell, your level of happiness.

When somebody has Success defined in the Graph with a Channel, it means they make time in their daily schedule for things that allow them to be successful in life. But it's not always about winning themselves, but also about helping others to succeed. Someone with Success and Sharing could be a teacher helping you to reach your goals. The definition of Success is the same as we saw it in the Triangle. It's still about getting ahead in life, succeeding with your job, winning at a sports competition, earning money and anything else you want to succeed in. It's about working hard for a goal.

The important difference to Feeling is that Success can continue doing things despite hardship and challenges. It can make sacrifices. It minds less if things are tough, as long is there is hope to succeed.

If someone has Feeling in their Triangles, this capacity is limited. They have to find a way that makes them feel good in regular intervals or they might quit.

When you look at all these numbers and themes in BaanTu that one person can have at the same time, you might wonder how it's possible to make them all work at the same time. But that's exactly what most of us do all day without even knowing. We all try to find a way to make it all work. And sometimes we quit things because it didn't work out. It's not a mistake. It's a process of elimination. Sometimes you cannot know these things in advance. And later you learn that the qualities that the Program is looking for are not there, you quit and start looking for something else. This doesn't just apply to activities or a job, it also applies to the people we work and live with. Life is a constant adjustment to what the Program wants from us.

I'm somebody who has a double Feeling Triangle. If the Program would not every once in a while switch on the Success Pressure Centre in my life, I would probably never do anything to be successful, which means working hard and making a few sacrifices. Of course I also have a few hanging Gate reaching out to Success, which means I don't have to be the one making sacrifices and suffer. I might do my part coming through Love, while the other person connecting with my Love Gate deals with the

Success aspect.

If I have Success temporarily activated by a planet (Transit), I would make a greater effort to push myself to the edges of my Feeling Triangle comfort zone. I might not be able to go as far as a Success Triangle, but might make at least a good effort. Without Success activated I would probably only indulge myself in feeling good all day, not even trying.

FEELING

Here we meet another old friend from the Triangles. Feeling is in many ways a mirror of Success. Even when you look at the Graph it looks like the mirror of the other side. At the same time it would be a grave mistake to think that these themes are mutually exclusive. Nobody says that it isn't possible to be successful and to feel good. It might just take a little longer to find a suitable activity, but worth the effort.

Sometimes you have people like me who have Feeling in the Triangles *and* the Pressure Centres, in which case you have to understand what a big part of their life "feeling good" is. These are incredibly emotional and sensitive beings. They are looking for good entertainment in life. They react immediately if something changes the way they *feel*. Good or bad. They wear their emotions on their sleeve. But they also have less time for other things in life. They are only motivated to do things that make them feel good.

Not everybody has such an extreme combination, many people have a mix of various themes. I will go through a couple of examples later in the book, which makes it easier to understand, but when you look at a person, you always begin with the Triangle to see what really matters for them. And it matters, because it's the thing that decides if they are miserable or happy. Having said that, this thing alone is not in control of what they actually want to do. It's an illusion. We are not aware that the Program has different tricks to make us do something. One is happiness, the other motivation. The Triangles and the Channels. They are not the same. One determines our mood, the other regulates our energy.

ENDURANCE

This Centre is a bit of a strange one, because it's not what some of you might think first. It's not about having more energy. And it's not about resilience or sensitivity.

What Endurance people are good at is that they don't quit the first time when things go wrong. They have this ability to stay with things longer despite failure. It's the Hexagon that tells us how sensitive a person is and the Triangle what their definition of failure is. The Circle finally shows how you implement your motivation. Do you initiate or do you wait for the right opportunity?

But no matter what you end up doing and how you go about it, when you fail and have Endurance defined, chances are bigger that you will try again (after a possible period of recovery).

A person with no Endurance is more likely to give up right away and try something else instead, if there are difficulties along the way.

As you can see in the Graph, Endurance is only available for three things in life: Success, Service and Feeling. It's where the Program is giving you a second chance, whereas with all the other themes it wants you to move on more quickly if things don't work out. It doesn't have as much patience with Love, Desire or Sharing. It doesn't want you to make the same mistake twice here.

TRIANGLE & HEXAGON

When you become more skilful with BaanTu, you'll start to master the art of reading several components together. First, when everything is new, you begin with a single component and interpret it in isolation. But the real fun begins when you can read them together, when you see how one thing influences the other, and both of them something else. It's a little bit like juggling oranges. You start with one and then, after a bit of training, you master keeping five of them in the air.

The sum of the components in BaanTu is much more than the individual components. They all interact with each other. It's like a chemical reaction of two substances. Something else, something bigger, emerges out of them.

The next logical step after looking at the Triangles and Hexagons separately would be to see them as a pair.

If you are someone with a Triangle-1 (Success) and a Hexagon-1, it means you have a low resilience to failure. Therefore you might tend to be a sore loser. Don't just read the Hexagon alone. You must look at the Triangle to see in more detail *what* you are sensitive about, or in what context you have a thick skin.

Therefore, we have people who are sensitive in various degrees to Success, Respect or Feeling. Some can take a "beating" and others not. The Triangles tells you *what* they are resilient against or not. And this in turn has an effect on their confidence and sensitivity towards others. It's impossible to know exactly how people will react out of these two number combinations. But when they do, you can start to understand what triggered it, you can see what the underlying reason was for their reaction.

A lower Hexagon will always try to control how exposed it is to the outside. It's uncomfortable to be at risk. It wants to have a "door" it can control to keep certain things and people away. But what it likes to control is the Triangle. If you want to be precise, it wants to control a situation, where it could get hurt by the theme of the Triangle.

EVEL KNIEVEL

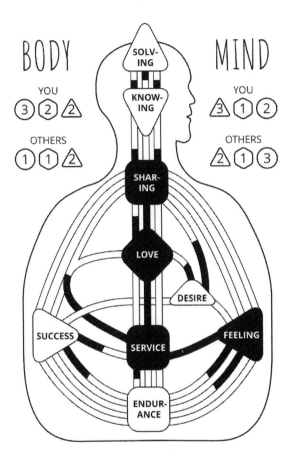

Let's look at a few examples to put into practice what we have learned so far. I love watching documentaries about famous people, especially if I have precise birth data for them. A few months ago, I was watching *I am Evel*

Knievel, a movie about the American stunt performer, crazy entertainer, and international icon. I vaguely remember him from my childhood and once saw him in a news program jumping over London double-decker buses with his bike. He got hurt many times and I was impressed by his determination, both physically and mentally.

When I first started watching the movie (not yet knowing his BaanTu data), I thought to myself that this guy must have a Circle-3 on the body in order to act this way. Circle-3's are always pushing the envelope. Luckily, I was able to get a precise birth time for him, and of course he had it, together with a Hexagon-2. This means that despite being in constant "attack" mode, he was realistic about his chances of getting hurt. I do remember some moments in the movie, one when he was about to jump over a canyon in a rocket and the other at Wembley Stadium where he wanted to break a record by jumping over those double-decker buses. You could see the fear and hesitation in him. There was something in him that said: "Do you really want to do this?"

Of course, a Hexagon-1 would have been petrified and probably not be in a profession like this in the first place. The constant fear would be almost unbearable. They also would be traumatised after the first accident.

A Circle-2 on the mind and a Circle-3 on the body means that he was an Opportunist with his mind, but physically he was pursuing and pushing things all the time. He was going after things from one to the next to the next. There is a kind of restlessness with Circle-3's. They think "waiting" is death. Knievel knew what he wanted. I wasn't surprised to hear that he had countless affairs with women and his wife was terribly upset about it. He also had high expectations on the material plane.

Before he began his stunt career, he was one of the best insurance salesmen, but also a great con man. No surprise with a 2/3 Circle. He could walk up to anyone, and when he saw an opportunity, "attack" with words and convince them.

Let's break down his data. On the body side, he had a Triangle-2 so his image and appearance were very important for him. You can see this in his iconic dress style and the image he created as Evel Knievel, down to that memorable name. A toy company had manufactured the Evel Knievel Stunt Cycle, which was one of the most sold toys at the time. It earned him millions and he had everything from houses, cars, and helicopters to his own jet, which fits with the Circle-3 that aims high on the material plane.

What the body side shows with the Triangle-2 is that he wanted to be respected, that he craved the applause. But he wasn't waiting for life to hand him an opportunity to be adored. He was an Initiator going at full throttle to get things. On the mind side, what he says (and how other people react) is judged by his feelings. He was known for his violent outbursts towards journalists at the canyon jump, which basically destroyed his career and led to the loss of everything he owned. He was an emotional speaker and thinker. People with a Triangle-3 mind combined with a thin skin (Hexagon-1) can't take criticism well and if people make them feel bad, they can lash out. Because he doesn't have a Success Triangle, there was nothing stopping him. He wasn't thinking about his career when journalists provoked him. It was purely an emotional response. But with his Hexagon-1, he was not a confident speaker, which tends to make things worse, because he probably felt even more threatened when verbally attacked. He hated being exposed to reporters asking him inconvenient questions. He probably feared reporters more than his stunts.

Looking at "others" on the body side, he liked to surround himself with people who were not as crazy as him. On the contrary, he liked Hexagon-1 and Circle-1 people, passive and sensitive people, aware of all the dangers. I have a hunch this combination saved his life in many situations. He had the right people around him.

When we look at his Pressure Centres, we get to the themes that motivated his actions. The first thing we see is Love to Sharing. The middle Channel of the three is something you usually see highlighted in a lot of creative performers. There is a deep need to share what one loves with the people. He loved riding his bikes. And he shared it with other people. But he also gave people what they loved. We also see the Channel right below, which is a nice extension of the same theme – again something you see with quite a few great artists. It's connects Service with Love and it means you do something that you love or people love, but also something that people want and ask for. He was very much aware of what people wanted to see and he delivered. He had a nose for commercial success. Finally, we have Service and Feeling, which are not only about him feeling good, but making other people feel good. Because it's connected to Service, it means you especially do what other people want. It's again a classic Channel of an entertainer, although there are many other possible examples.

We haven't covered this yet, but he also had two Channels in the leadership category, which doesn't mean he wanted to be a leader, but rather that people easily followed him. This explains his popularity and iconic status.

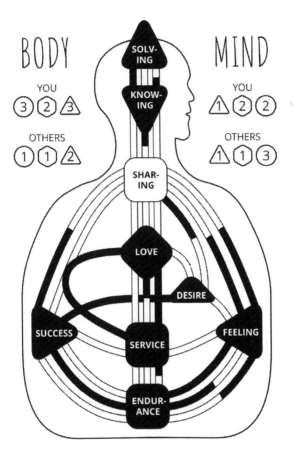

When I watched the movie about Evel Knievel, I noticed the presenter of the documentary was Johnny Knoxville from the *Jackass* film series. When I saw a few clips about Knoxville at the end of the Knievel movie,

I thought: This guy is almost like Evel Knievel! Surely, he must have similar numbers. They acted like twins.

Again, I was lucky and found a precise birth time. Not only do they both have the same Hexagon and Circle on the body, but also the same Circle on the mind. But I could see Knoxville had better control over what he says, and yes, he has a Triangle-1, Success, on the mind so wouldn't say anything bad for his career. He is also a more confident speaker with the Hexagon-2 on the mind.

An interesting side note is that he (similar to Evel) likes to surround himself with Hexagon-1 and Circle-1 people on the body side, which acts as a little life insurance if you are on the wilder side like they both are.

With Johnny though there is a slight difference. He is less creative, and not so much concerned about his image, but very much driven by Success. Creativity is something we learn in the Circuits chapter. He has Success in the Triangle as well as in the Graph where he has it combined with Endurance and Desire. That's quite a combination. To succeed in life is paramount for him. This is not the same as with Evel. Somebody with Success might care about winning at any cost more than what people think about them. They can almost prostitute themselves for Success. They are incredibly competitive, and they don't care what other people think of them. For Evel, on the other hand, what people thought about him was his primary motivation – it made him happy.

JUAN MANUEL FANGIO

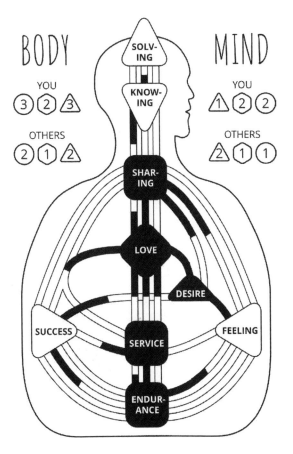

BODY

MIND

YOU
③ ② ③

YOU
① ② ②

OTHERS
② ① ②

OTHERS
② ① ①

SOLV-
ING

KNOW-
ING

SHAR-
ING

LOVE

DESIRE

SUCCESS

SERVICE

FEELING

ENDUR-
ANCE

L et's stay with the theme of daredevils. Juan Manuel Fangio is regarded by many as the greatest Formula One driver of all time. I actually met him when I was a child. My grandfather was close friends with the Mercedes

Benz racing director Alfred Neubauer, who was one of the most iconic figures in early F1 racing. I remember some famous F1 drivers staying in my grandfather's picturesque summer house on a hill in Austria's Wachau. Neubauer was the greatest story teller I met. Most people today have no idea how dangerous F1 used to be. It wasn't unusual for several people to die on a single weekend. The cars were incredibly difficult to drive, yet very powerful and fast. They were heavy monsters and the racing courses were death traps. One little mistake and you were dead.

Fangio was called *El Maestro*, dominating F1 like no other. His record for World Championships stood for 47 years and was only beaten by Michael Schumacher. Fangio still holds the highest winning percentage in F1. He won 24 of 53 races he entered.

Again, we see the Hexagon-2 and Circle-3 combination on the body side. Maximum attack (Initiator) on the body side, always pushing, with a realistic assessment of danger. But we also see a Triangle-1 for Success on the mind side. This guy wanted to win. It was in his blood. And as all 2/3 (mind/body) Circles, he was incredibly popular with women. He was a womanizer with a string of girlfriends. At **baantu.com,** you can search people, including more than 1,000 celebrities, with any of these numbers. Wildcard characters (*) are allowed. To search for Circle-3 on the body and Circle-2 on the mind, you type 3**–**2 into the search box of the people directory.

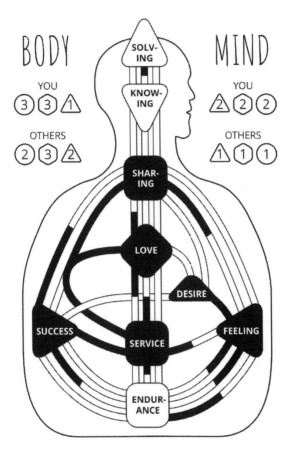

Here is another one of the great F1 drivers. I chose him for several reasons. First, he is originally from Austria like me and I met him twice. As a kid I had a poster with his autograph in my room. More importantly, he was very successful and won the World Championship twice, also at a time when driving was a constant fight with death. Another reason I chose him is the movie *Rush* (2013) centred on the rivalry between Lauda and James Hunt (who is also in the BaanTu library). The movie gives readers like yourself an excellent opportunity to study the examples I chose and learn what you see in BaanTu. It's how all these numbers and Centres from the Graph come alive.

Arguably, the most memorable event in Lauda's racing career was his terrible accident at the infamous Nürburgring in Germany, at one time called "the Green Hell". He was the only person to lap the 22.8 km long Nordschleife in under seven minutes and was the reigning World Champion when he crashed his Ferrari. His car burst into flames and he was trapped inside. He was saved by fellow drivers rather than by the ill-equipped track marshals, who, due to the long track distance, were too far away.

He suffered severe burns to his head and inhaled hot toxic gases that damaged his lungs and blood. As Lauda was wearing a modified helmet, the foam had compressed and it slid off his head after the accident, leaving his face exposed to the fire. Although Lauda was conscious and able to stand immediately after the accident, he later lapsed into a coma. He suffered extensive scarring from the burns to his head, losing most of his right ear as well as the hair on the right side of his head, his eyebrows, and his eyelids. He later chose to limit reconstructive surgery to replacing the eyelids and getting them to work properly. Since the accident he had always worn a cap to cover the scars on his head.

In the hospital, he fought with death for four days. His chances for survival were slim. Worse than his terrible burns, several broken ribs, and cheekbone fracture were his damaged lungs that got burned by the toxic gases.

What you might find really hard to believe is that six weeks later he was back in the racing car, peeling the blood-soaked bandages off his scarred scalp in the pits. Only a Hexagon-3 can do that.

I think you have a pretty good idea about the person by now. It will come as no surprise to see he has a Circle-3 and a Hexagon-3 on the body side. This man knows how to attack and is fearless, some might say unrealistic. You also see that it can get people into deep trouble. Coupled with this is also a Triangle-1 on the body. This is someone has no fear and is determined to win. A Triangle-1 can even switch off the emotions if they need to.

On the mind side, he wants to be respected (Triangle-2) and craved popularity and admiration. Later in life, he became a pilot and owner of two commercial airlines.

James Hunt, on the other hand, had a reputation as a playboy. He wasn't motivated by praise. If you look at his data at **baantu.com**, he had two Triangle-3's. He wanted to enjoy himself in life. He didn't give a damn what other people thought and he had no huge desire to win. He only wanted to have fun. But you can also see that he had a Hexagon-3 on the body side. First of all that made him fearless, and also very confident with his own body. There are many pictures of Hunt with a naked upper body. That guy wasn't shy. And he used his confidence to have fun. He wasn't into F1 to succeed. He was in it for the fun. He probably lacked the discipline Lauda had.

Lauda used his high confidence primarily to win and worked much harder than Hunt. He had a Success Triangle plus a defined Success Pressure Centre. He was also (like Hunt) very confident with his physical appearance, but had a Triangle-2 only on the mind side, not the body so he didn't care what other people thought about his scars and deformities. It explains why he wasn't much concerned about reconstructive surgery after the accident. By the way, his physical appearance after his accidents didn't stop him from having plenty of affairs, even when he was older. He was a party goer and was often seen in night clubs surrounded by girls.

AYRTON SENNA

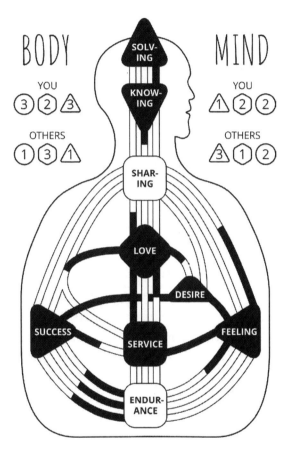

Here we come to another Formula One icon. He won three World Championships and is also regarded as one of the greatest drivers of all time. He died in an accident in 1994 due to a mechanical failure.

As with all the other F1 drivers so far, we again see a Circle-3 on the body, aiming high and going after things physically. His Hexagon is a 2, making him realistic with assessments of what can go wrong. But so far, we have not seen a Hexagon-1 with the drivers. I guess being too cautious would slow them down too much. But most importantly, we haven't seen anything lower than a Circle-3 on the body side. They must act aggressive, with purpose. They don't wait for opportunities, they create them. If you want to win, you have to go after things. You always attack. You don't wait for people to hand you a trophy. You go and get it.

In addition, we see a double Success theme, one in the mind Triangle and another one in the Graph connected to Desire. This man had a strong desire to win. That was what made him happy and it was also his focus and motivation. At the same time, he was attracted to people who were fearless, some might say careless (Hexagon-3).

As with all men who are popular with women, he had the irresistible 2/3 (mind/body) Circle combination. The Triangle-3 on the body gave him great emotional depth and sensitivity. These people often come across as warm and friendly, in touch with their emotions, which explains why he was so incredibly popular as a person, not just for his success, but for his character.

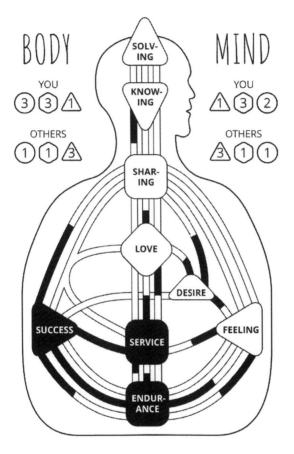

Here we come to the last in our mini-series of Formula One's greatest drivers. I don't think I have to introduce Schumacher to many of you. He is the only driver in history to win seven World Championships, which makes him the most successful driver in the history of the sport.

Similar to Niki Lauda we see the highest risk combination on the body side with a Hexagon-3 and Circle-3. These people just don't know fear, have no intention of acting cautiously, and have high expectations. After all, they know what they want and go after it. With Schumacher, we also see something we didn't have with the previous drivers. We have a *quadruple* Success theme, combined with Endurance.

He has a Triangle-1, both on the body and mind. Every cell in his body wants to win. Winning decides if he is happy or not. I guess you won't easily find a more competitive person. In addition (as if this wasn't already enough), he is under pressure with two Channels going to Success in the Graph. One is combined with Endurance, the other with Service (giving people what they want). Of course, people wanted him to win because he cared about his fans. This man had a lot of them all over the world.

Yet, so much (over)confidence, competitive pressure, and the need for adventure often comes at a price. In December 2013, Schumacher suffered a traumatic brain injury in a skiing accident. While crossing an unsecured off-piste area, he fell and hit his head on a rock, sustaining a serious head injury. He was placed in a medically induced coma for six months. Little is known about his condition. Some reports said that he is paralysed, in a wheelchair, can't speak, and has memory problems.

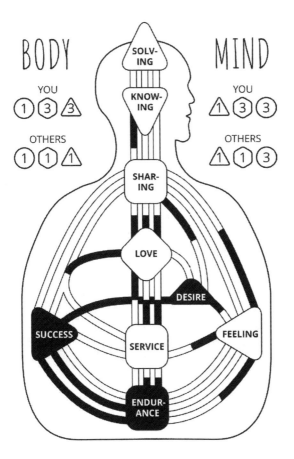

For our final example, before we continue with the principles of BaanTu, we make a little theme change from the daredevils to one of the most successful musicians of our current time, Taylor Swift.

The reason I picked her was because of the *Taylor Swift: Just For You* documentary I saw on YouTube. I love documentaries when you have a precise birth time for a person. You learn so much about the Graph.

Swift is not just a very successful young artist and performer, she is also a prolific songwriter. What you see with many musicians, especially singers and writers, is that they have a Triangle-3 on the body. They are emotionally sensitive due to their need to feel good. Because of this, they also have a gift to make other people feel good through their songs and voice.

But what's really startling with Swift is the sheer dominance of Success in her Graph. First you see it in her mind Triangle, then you see three Channels going to Success, two from Endurance and one from Desire. This is probably the strongest Success combination I have ever seen in a person and makes her one of the hardest working people in the business. But if that isn't enough, she also has two Success Triangles in "others", which means she prefers to surround herself with hard-working people who put everything else second in life. She is not interested in time-wasters. She wants people around her to live and breathe Success. And if all that still isn't enough, she has the highest confidence a person can have: A double Hexagon-3. The interesting thing is that she has a Circle-1 where she prefers to respond instead of bothering and physically "attacking" people. The Hexagon-3 though makes her unafraid of people and she doesn't hide. She loves to be invited. She is patient with people, able to wait for the right person to come along. She is not pursuing people. People come to her. She is known to be very much in touch with her fans, willing to sign autographs all day. She is not building walls around herself and is very confident in her own physical body and capabilities.

On the mind side, she has a double 3 with the Hexagon-3 and Circle-3. Now this is different from the body. First, Circle-3/Hexagon-3 minds always dream big. They know what they want and they go after it. They have high aspirations in life. But she can also be very convincing, which was evident when she was constantly knocking at the doors of record labels in Nashville and trying to convince them to give her a record contract at the age of 15. They rejected her and sent her away, but she kept coming back, which is something that her double Endurance is responsible for. But another important aspect is her double Hexagon-3, which makes her very resilient to rejection and criticism. She has a thick skin and isn't traumatized by failure. We also know that Hexagon-3's can be insensitive and she is known to write about her ex-boyfriends in her songs.

She herself said: "Being in this business means to be competitive and restless." People who know her said that she refuses for anything to stand in the way of her dreams. She has a sign in her tour bus that says "Never give up!"

That's what a double Endurance and triple Success definition does.

Another interesting thing is the lack of any Channel or Gates between Solving and Knowing. Even between Knowing and Sharing, there is only one meagre Gate. That shows you that the Program doesn't pressure Swift to spend a lot of time in her life thinking about things or figuring them out. She is less of an intellectual and more of a "doer". This is not an indication of how smart someone is, but rather a sign that you spend less time using your mind for things that could have a value for others.

LIFE GATES

Not all the Gates in the Graph are equal. There are four of them that are more important than the rest. They are defined by the position of the Sun and Earth at your moment of birth and the three months before that. We've already heard about the 13 celestial bodies for the body and mind side, resulting in a total of 26 Gates.

When you look at the illustration to the right, four Gates are highlighted. These Gates define the Life Role of a person, they tell us what the most important things are in their life. Every one of these Life Gates is connected to a

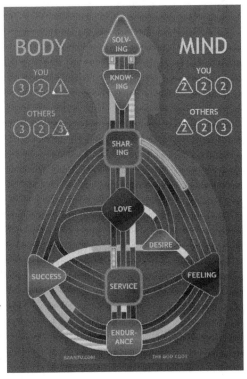

143

Pressure Centre, which also becomes highlighted.

The above-example is that of the actress Evan Rachel Wood, known for her role as Dolores in *Westworld*. You can load her data onto **baantu.com** to see more. What's interesting to notice is that two of her highlighted Gates are in undefined Centres. It is a trap and oversight to judge a person without looking at their Life Gates. Just because a Centre is not defined in your birth Graph doesn't mean it's not important. On the contrary. It just means it might not always be active. We already know that there are several additional ways to activate a hanging Gate and, with that, possibly an undefined Centre. It's either by the Transit (the current position of the 13 celestial bodies) or by interacting with another person who has the Gate on the other side of one of your hanging Gates.

When we look at Wood, we see two of her Life Gates coming down from the Solving Centre, which makes this the most important thing in her life followed by Sharing and Service, each having one Life Gate.

Service and Sharing aren't defined in her birth Graph and would have been missed if we didn't highlight her Life Gates activated from the Sun and Earth.

When, for example, Service and Sharing are not defined but highlighted, this is something very important in your life, but just not always available. It's like the Program gives you a break every once in a while from that pressure. To get a better picture, you must look at the Life Gates to see if they form a full Channel or are just hanging Gates. It's enough if a Life Gate forms a Channel with another one of your Gates. You don't need two Life Gates to form a Channel. In Wood's case, her Gate at the top left coming down from Solving is also a Channel. This means that it's always available throughout her life. She neither needs anyone else to live it out nor does she have to wait for a Transit (this is indicated by a red bolt symbol on the [EASY] page). But her other three Life Gates are hanging. In order for her to get a chance to live them out, she has to wait for the right moment or person to switch them on.

You can clearly see Wood is not a person who blindly accepts information. She will always try to solve and think about things on her own. She has her own mind, but by having Desire, she can also be incredibly stubborn. At the same time with having both Sharing and Service as her Life Centres, she has a very sharing side and also wants to know what other people's needs are. She might be stubborn and it's important for her to do only the things she wants to do (you can't make her do things), but at the same time, she is paying attention to what other people want, but not always. Service and Sharing are not always defined, but when they are, she feel these pressures and those themes become very important for her.

RELATIONSHIPS

Here is one of the most popular features on baantu.com. I don't think there is anything else in the world right now that can give you such accurate and consistent information about the nature of a relationship between two people.

With BaanTu, you can not only browse people in your own private library, but also every registered user and more than 1,000 celebrities. You can browse registered users by name, city, county, and country. As you browse, a "star-rating" for the relationship automatically appears with you next to their picture. In addition, you can see how another

person ticks the six qualities you're looking for (from "others" in your Graph). There is a little dot underneath the Circle, Hexagon, and Triangle to let you know if a person has what you are looking for (from your "others" row). If you see a cross, it means this quality is slightly annoying for you, because you are neither looking for this quality nor are you compatible with it (you don't have it yourself). Yet, the dots and crosses are only one aspect of many in the relationship calculation, which explains why you could have a high star-rating with less dots, but also a low star-rating with many dots.

The star-rating in the people directory (the illustration above, where you browse all the people) is always calculated relative to the data of the account owner. For this reason, it's important that you never change your own birth data by accident.

What does the star-rating tell you? It doesn't tell you who the right person is for you. This is something only you can know. There are many other factors that decide this – factors BaanTu can't track. Of course, BaanTu neither shows physical attractiveness between two people nor tracks the mystery of "love". What it can see is if the other person has characteristics that you generally like in others. It also reveals whether the other person's characteristics are compatible with your own, plus there are a few other factors that we'll delve into later in this chapter.

But first, what is it all for?

It's not about changing the other person or yourself. BaanTu is never about that. This is not a life or relationship "coach". It's not a tool that offers fixes. Remember, BaanTu is merely a microscope into our nature. You see for yourself what can't be changed because certain factors are outside human control. By living a life of "trying to change them" though, you risk destroying the relationship. Instead you should learn to *manage* whatever the relationship is. Learn to work *with* it, rather than fight it. You can't change the influence of the Program. You can't change how the Bhan aspects of dark matter control us. They want you to be with certain kinds of people so the universe can be healthy. Life is an organism that must follow certain patterns that humans are not allowed to disrupt.

The star-rating essentially shows how much time you want to spend with a specific person. A low star-rating is not the end of the world. It doesn't mean the person is "bad" for you. It only means that after a certain amount of time, the Program will remind you that you have other things to do and this person is holding you back from those tasks or activities. When people have a low star-rating with you, after a while they either begin to annoy you or you are beginning to annoy them. Don't take it too personally or too black and white. There is no perfect relationship.

If you have a higher star-rating, it's possible to spend more time with them, because they probably help you get where the Program wants you to go. But not everyone who has a five star-rating is the "right" person for you. Theoretically, it's just possible for you to spend more time with them. There are other factors like the Magnetic Monopole, which is the control mechanism deciding who the right people are in your life. The star-rating will tell you how much or little time you spend with each of them.

To look at a relationship in more detail, you have to load one person into slot [A] and the other into slot [B] by clicking the [A][B] switch. Whenever you initially load **baantu.com**, it loads your own data into slot [A] and [B], so all you have to do to see a relationship is to load another person into the already active slot. Next you switch from single [👤] to relationship mode [👥] to see the relationship information.

Above [A][B] you see a switch for [EASY] and [GRAPH]. I recommend that you begin with the [EASY] mode, as it gives you the essential information.

While you are limited within the people directory (menu) to only see star-ratings relative to yourself, you can load *anybody* into [A] and [B] to see the relationship rating between any two people stored at **baantu.com**. Of course, you can store your own people if you know their birth times. People who you store with [SAVE] can *not* be seen by anyone else. Only the main account holder's data is shared (without revealing the birth data to others). None of the data is indexed by search engines like Google and data of the account holder can only be seen by other registered users, who also have to share their own data under the motto: "I show you mine, if you show me yours."

There is nothing in the data that one has to be ashamed about or might be used against you. What's "good" for one person is always "bad" for someone and vice-versa. Also, I think it's wonderful if people can understand you better and see what's important for you and what makes you unhappy or triggers a reaction. They might be able to work better with you, because they get how you tick. It's really never about "changing" another person or oneself. It's about understanding and trying to work with who we are.

The first relationship quality to notice on BaanTu is how compatible a person is with another. Compatibility is not always the most obvious quality. The "sparks" that fly when you meet someone are usually coming from the "attraction" quality, which we also measure in BaanTu.

Compatibility, on the other hand, looks at all of your own qualities, including your numbers in the four Hexagons, four Circles, and four Triangles, and compares them with those from the other person. I also look at other aspects in the Graph, like Gates, Channels, Centres, and Life Gates to see how *similar* both people are. The more similarities there are, the greater the understanding about what the other person does and wants, but especially how they go about getting things done.

Compatibility is not what we are "looking" for in another person. Rather, that is "attraction", the result of the two Hexagons, Circles and Triangles we have in "others" in the Graph, illustrated by the rows of green LED's on the [EASY] [👥] page, followed by the "attractive" meter.

In the end, neither of the two (attraction and compatibility) work well in extremes on their own. I think it helps to have a bit of both for a relationship. The best attraction might not have much of a future if you are totally incompatible, and the highest compatibility is boring if the other person doesn't have qualities you're looking for.

The rows of LED's that you see under A and B, next to the Hexagons, Circles, and Triangles indicate whether a person has qualities desired by the other. It basically shows what one person has in the Graph under "others" and whether this matches what the other person has in "you".

Compared with "compatibility", this is not a mutual quality. One person can be much more attractive to the other than vice-versa. The number of green LED's are controlling the attraction meter underneath, telling you if this person is attractive with their various qualities (Hexagon, Triangle or Circle) to the other.

When an LED is red, it means that this quality in the person is not only unattractive, but also incompatible (not the same to what the other person has). There are three options with other people's qualities:

1) They have what you are looking for in another person (green light).

2) They don't have what you are looking for, but are compatible with you (no light).

3) They don't have what you are looking for and also aren't compatible (red light). The red light is shown as a small x in the people directory and the green light as small dot under the six symbols to give you an overview when browsing.

Let's talk about another aspect for relationships. You already know from the chapter about the Pressure Centres that there are three possible ways a Channel can be formed. The ones in your "default" Graph were formed based on the position of the planets at birth.

In addition to that, we add the current position of the planets (Transit), which will activate more Gates and possibly more Channels.

The third possible activation comes from other people whose Gates connect to your hanging Gates. Any activation is always felt as an increased motivation to do certain things. If you look at your Graph, you have hanging Gates that don't form Channels. When two people meet with hanging Gates that can form a Channel, they become active. This is when additional pressure or motivation towards certain activities are suddenly felt. This is a mutual quality that both parties experience.

Interestingly, we recognise this in strangers when we meet them. I have no idea how nature allows us to recognize this, but if you meet a person with the possibility of making a lot of connections to your hanging Gates, this person can pique your interest just by standing at the other side of a room full of people, even before you have a chance to talk to them or know more about them.

But let's be clear: A Channel doesn't get activated by *standing* next to them. You have to *do* things together, you have to interact, for the motivation of the Channel to be felt and expressed. The difference with a relationship Channel is that every party is only motivated by their side of the bargain, *their* Centre. But this Centre can only be used with the other side of the Channel (and the other Centre) when the other person brings that into the relationship, like sharing a task.

When you look at the "total" meter in the "additional motivation" section, you see the addition motivation one feels within the relationship. Usually this is mutual.

Now here comes the catch: In the chapter before, we talked about the Life Gates and how important they are in our lives.

If you look at the black boxes on the relationship page

showing red numbers, this is the influence of the Life Gates within relationships.

The "additional motivation" section shows you how many of your Life Gates are activated by the other person. Since both people within a relationship usually have *different* Life Gates, this is not always mutual. All of a sudden the motivation might be bigger for one person than the other. By looking at the red numbers you can see if one person motivates more than the other. If the numbers are equal then the motivation is mutually felt.

The meters underneath the "total" meter break the motivation down into various themes that we will discuss in the next (Circuits) chapter.

Finally, we come to the "dominance" meters. Most of the time there is nothing nice about dominance. It means that the one person never gets their way, that they feel ignored. The higher the dominance is, the more aspects (Gates) in the Graph are affected by dominance.

Dominance in BaanTu means one person has the whole Channel, while the other only has a hanging Gate within that Channel. It means that the person with the whole Channel is controlling everything and never gives the other person a chance to live out their Gate. The other person is robbed of their Gate.

Dominance is not a mutual value, therefore it's possible for one person to dominate the other more, but not vice-versa. Dominance is not something that you necessarily notice right away, especially if the attraction is high, and impressions and admiration are strong. It might be okay in a teacher-student relationship. Not every kind of dominance is a huge problem. It only is when both parties expect to be equals or spend a lot of time together.

At the beginning of a relationship, when we meet, we are more forgiving. But dominance is the carbon monoxide of relationships. It's a silent killer. The danger is that the person dominating the other is usually not aware of it and may not even be remotely conscious of the effects of their actions, because dominance isn't mutual. BaanTu is helpful in this regard. You can see if you are dominating somebody, although it's difficult to do something about it. Sometimes the best thing you can do is to give the other person a bit of breathing space from the relationship.

Another classic mistake with "dominance" is to think when both parties have equal amounts of it that it is okay. It's not. It just means both sides are dominant in different areas and it makes the relationship worse. It doesn't "balance out". Now instead of one, there are two people complaining or feeling trampled over. Whenever a person is dominated, there is a growing anger and frustration that builds up over time.

Similar to the "additional motivation", we can also look under "dominance" at how our very important Life Gates are affected. If you have your Life Gate defined as a Channel in your own Graph, then you are immune against being dominated by anyone else here. You also don't need other people to live out your Life Gates. You don't depend on others to activate them nor can they block you with dominance.

When somebody dominates your Life Gate (Role), this is often one of the worst things that can happen to you. It happens when you have a hanging Life Gate and the other person has the whole Channel including that Gate. The black boxes with the red numbers will show you how many of your Life Gates the other person dominates for the mind and body aspects of your Life Role.

What we can't see within the relationship page is "love". If you read my other book *The Prophecy of Ra Uru Hu*, you will hear that "love" is the by-product of the Magnetic Monopole and also has to do with a hierarchy established at the Big Bang when the Bhan Crystal shattered into countless aspects.

All the Bhan aspects, sitting in living forms and influencing them, have a relationship that is invisible to us. Yet, it's the Magnetic Monopole within us that determines what we experience as "love" to tell us who the "right" people and places are in our lives. This is something separate from the star-rating at **baantu.com**. First, you need to have the right people in your life, which the Monopole controls and we feel as "love". Then the star-rating or influences of the Bhan aspects controlling our mind and body determine how much time we spend with the people in our lives.

CIRCUITS

Here we come to another layer of information about the Channels in the Graph. You might already have wondered why some of the Pressure Centres have more than one possible connection (Channel) to each other. Many of them have three, some even four like Sharing/Love and Service/Love.

A Circuit is similar to a machine that is built out of many components. Every component does its job, but some of them together fulfil an even larger task.

Most Channels belong to a larger Circuit, with only three of them working on their own. They don't belong to any Circuit. They don't have a larger theme they serve.

To understand a Circuit better, always look at the defined and undefined Centres it has.

The four Circuits are:

+ Collective Feeling
+ Collective Success
+ Creativity
+ Community

COMMUNAL CIRCUIT

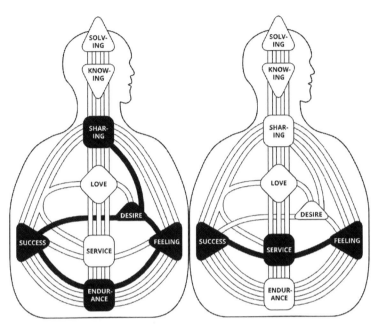

This Communal Circuit is the bedrock of any community, no matter if it's the family, the village, work, or what you do in your spare time with a group of people. It's about building and maintaining communities and involves regular and personal contact with people known well.

The Communal Circuit consists of two sub-circuits. The overall theme for both sub-circuits is, of course, the support of communities. Every community is built upon and functions with the help of promises, support, and bargain making. It's like a contract, which forms the foundations of any community. It's the understanding that one hand washes another. If you break the contract, the community will punish or expel you.

To understand a Channel in the Graph, it's always best to first consider what Circuit it belongs to, in order to understand the bigger picture.

Circuits do describe the kind of activity, but more than that, they can tell you who you are doing it for. Once that's established, you go deeper with the Channel itself and the Centres on both ends. The real trick then is to see it all together. All the different Channels, Circuits, Centres, Hexagons, Triangles, and Circles at once. When you become adept at interpretation, a story will emerge.

When someone has a Channel belonging to the Communal Circuit, the activity is always connected to people of a community. It's not about being alone and not involved personally. For example, I have very little "Communal" in my Graph. For me, to be part of a community and all its rules feels suffocating. I don't care so much about people's personal problems, I don't want to be a member of some kind of village club that meets every week. I'm not much of a "community guy". The community has very strict rules and obligations, and if you don't follow them, if you don't live up to your bargain, you are in trouble. It doesn't matter if it's the family or the European Union.

When you look at the Centres not part of the Communal Circuits, there is no Knowing or Solving. Looking at the defined as well as undefined Centres of a Circuit always helps in better understanding it. The Community doesn't think about things. It's about doing your job and fulfilling one's obligations. It also doesn't care about Love, which means they can't just do the things they love. The community used to arrange marriages, and in some parts of the world still does. You have to look after your family and sick members of the community, no matter if you love them or not. The community doesn't care. Being inside of a community is like having a contract. It's about support. There is no place for what you think or what you love. There is only what needs to be done and what other people need, depending on which of the sub-circuits the Channel belongs to. One has the emphasis of Desire, the other on Service.

Instead of over-explaining this, it's best to think about the Centres in the Circuit (and the lack of them) when you watch a person who has a Channel from the Community. They will give you another layer of understanding on top of the Channel itself with its connection to the two Centres. It's an art form to read all these different layers together.

A big part of the Channels for the community is based on making and spending money for the community. One is driven by Success, the other by Feeling. They make sure the community succeeds, but they also make sure its people feel good.

Communities are not good at Sharing. Compared with the other Circuits, it only has one connection to Sharing and this goes to Desire. It means that the community only shares what it wants to share. They can be hoarders. You can't "make" them share. Real sharing is not based on a bargain. It doesn't expect anything back in return. The community can also be stubborn (Desire Centre). And it can be unreasonable, with the lack of Knowing and Solving. Everything is based on "I scratch your back if you scratch mine." If you don't, they threaten to cast you out. People with Channels from this Circuit expect you to return a favour. They also need to be part of a Community to flourish. They don't want to live alone on a desert island.

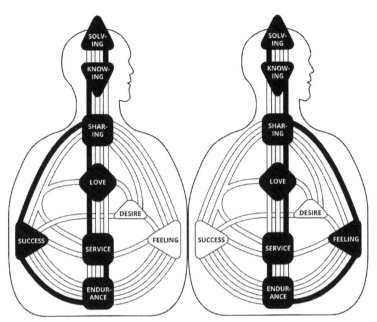

When you see a Circuit, the first thing it usually tells you is who you are working for, what that activity of a Channel is for. The Communal Circuit is all about supporting, building, and maintaining the community. The Collective Circuit, as the name already implies, serves the collective. Many times you don't know the people who you are working for on a personal basis. You might deal with strangers with one of these Channels whereas with the Communal Circuit one usually has personal relationships and sees them on a regular basis.

Think about a member of parliament. They usually can't spend their time meeting every citizen and listening to all their individual problems. They are primarily interested in things that can improve the lives of *many*, not just one. But most of all, they are not in the business of bargains like the community is. The Collective Circuit doesn't wait for a favour to be returned.

To highlight the differences between the Communal and Collective Circuits in the context of BaanTu, you must understand that someone with a Communal Channel feels motivated to contribute towards the community. In order to build and maintain communities, a person is bound by their rules, contracts, and bargains. There are many obligations that the community demands and wants. That's also how people with these Channels "tick".

People with Collective Channels don't have the same closeness, they are not as "thick" as the community. There is not the "I scratch your back if you scratch mine" mentality and possible punishment if you don't. The Collective can be more aloof, but also doesn't expect a favour to be returned. The Collective is more like a freelancer, but it still has intentions to improve the life of others. It comes with freedom, but also less guaranteed support, less entitlement. The Community, on the other hand, feels more like fixed employment with rights.

A musician who gives a concert for a larger crowd, especially if they don't personally know the audience, serves the collective. The same goes for a journalist for a larger newspaper or TV station, or a book writer. Their work is for the many. Even when they talk to one person, they usually don't do so just for the sake of that individual's story, but to glean information from the conversation that is relevant to share with their audience, to the wider world on a collective basis. It's not tailor-made for one.

If you look at both Success and Feeling Collective Circuits, they both miss Desire. It's undefined and left out. So if you have a Collective Channel, it's not usually about what *you* want. The Collective Circuit is not about being stubborn.

The difference between the two sub-circuits is that one is driven by Success and the other by Feeling.

This is, in fact, very easy to understand. You either help the collective to succeed or you make sure it feels good. You could also turn it around and say that one succeeds by working for the collective, or one does something or works to make them feel good. In a nutshell, whatever you do has to be connected with the collective.

When you look, for example, at the three Channels connecting Solving and Knowing, two of them are for serving the collective. One is to *succeed*, the other to *feel good*. Simply speaking, this means that if you want to solve something and have the Feeling Collective Circuit Channel, you can only mentally solve or mentally work on something that makes the collective feel good.

CREATIVE CIRCUIT

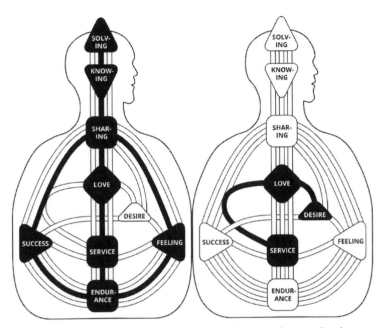

Here, with this Circuit, it's less about *who* we do things for, but more about *what* we do. This Circuit is responsible for bringing new things into the world. These Channels are responsible for innovation and creativity. They are the driving force of mutation.

Neither the Communal nor Collective Circuits invent new things. They might improve things, but they are not creative. Everyone who is creative knows that you can't control creativity. It has its own rhythm and timing. Melancholia is an important part of being creative.

Melancholy is the result of the waiting, of surrendering to the forces responsible for something new to miraculously emerge out of nothing. Only someone who doesn't have creative Channels themselves might confuse melancholy with depression. Melancholy is not sadness.

Mutation in nature also doesn't happen gradually. It always happens in leaps. Nothing might happen for a long time, and then all of a sudden something new emerges. Homo sapiens didn't gradually emerge. The Neanderthal didn't gradually morph into Homo sapiens.

The Creative Circuit doesn't have the same obligations as the Collective and the Communal ones. The Creative Circuit works for no one but itself. That's why they sometimes can be seen as "loose cannons" or "unpredictable" by communities or the collective. A creative person doesn't make promises, which can infuriate the community. At the same time, their inventions are important for humankind. If someone has Sharing from this Circuit, they feel motivated to share their creativity or inventions. This Circuit makes sure (with all the defined Centres you see) that it not only shares with others people, but also makes them feel good, helps them to succeed, and pays attention to what people want (Service).

NO CIRCUIT

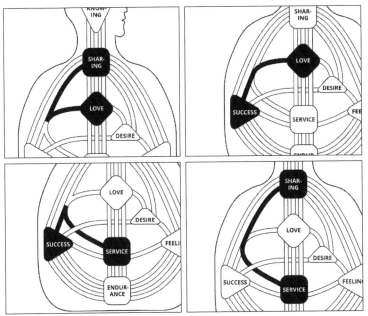

We have four Channels that don't belong to any Circuit. They have no "higher responsibility". The only responsibility the Program demands of them is that they look after themselves. These Channels are survival machines. They ensure our species doesn't die out in times of crisis.

The biggest difference compared with Channels connected to Circuits is that they don't have any obligation to the community, the collective, or creativity. They operate outside of these larger themes, which also means that they are going to put their own interests first.

While this doesn't mean they won't help others, they can only do this if they are secure and well-off themselves first, or you could say, they help you as long as it doesn't infringe on their own quality of life.

We see the themes of Sharing, Love, and Service here, so it's not like they never make contributions, but you must understand the conditions that this comes with. People with these Channels sometimes have to do things for themselves, despite what anyone else wants. They can be very direct and occasionally what other Circuits would describe as "selfish". They don't see the point of suffering for others, at least not on the same scale as people with Channels from other Circuits. If they suffer, they like to suffer for their own benefit.

MOTIVATION METERS

You can see meters for your motivation on the [EASY] page for you alone [👤] or in relationship mode [👥]. These meters look at all active Channels and break down the result into various themes. For example, it looks at how many Channels in a Graph are mental (above Sharing) and how many are physical (below Sharing). There is also a total count of Channels. If you compare your meters with other people's, you will discover that some are more motivated to do things than others. But don't forget that

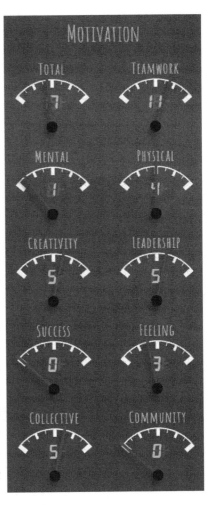

the default data (using the birth time only) doesn't tell the whole story. Some people don't have a lot of Channels defined with their birth time, but when you add the Transit (current position of planets) you will discover that the motivation increases considerably.

To add the Transit information, press one of the period buttons labelled 48 hours, week, month, or half year. BaanTu will then look at when, and for how long, various Channels  are active over the selected period. When these buttons are pressed in the [GRAPH] mode, you will see all the active Channels over that period. The ones active for longer are brighter than the ones active for a shorter period. You can use your mouse and hover over a Channel to see how long it is active. When it says 100%, you know it's active for the whole time of the selected period.

Some meters check if Channels belong to a Circuit, and in addition look which Centres are activated by Channels, such as in the case of "Feeling" and "Success". These two meters look the Collective Success and Feeling Circuit, but how many Channels are connected to the Success or Feeling centres, irrelevant of their Circuit.

On the relationship page [👥] you will see the additional motivation meters between two people. This is in addition to what you see on the page for yourself [👤].

*

In the single person mode [EASY][👤], there is a meter labelled "Teamwork". This is a ratio of your total defined Channels versus your total hanging Gates. More defined Channels means you are motivated to do things solo. Hanging Gates increase the motivation to look for another person so you can make use of your hanging Gates. Some people have lots of hanging Gates and not a lot of active Channels. Others have it the other way round. Of course, when you press the period buttons for the Transit, you might get more defined Channels, therefore the motivation for teamwork decreases. There are times when you are more motivated to work with others and then there are times when you are less motivated. But it's also obvious that some people are more open to teamwork than others.

The "Leadership" meter requires a bit of additional explanation, because it is not what you initially might think. It is not a motivation for you to become a leader. It also doesn't show if someone is a "good" or "bad" leader. Again, BaanTu can't tell if someone is "good" or "bad" at something. There are many ways how people can lead. This meter is the by-product of activated Channels in the centre column of the Graph. If any of the six Channels from Sharing down to Service in the centre column are activated, others will be more prone to follow that person. It's the kind of leader-ship that isn't enforced on others. Some of the people who have these Channels might not even want to be a leader, but they still inspire others by example. Other people want to follow them. Sometimes this can go to extremes where they'd do anything for them, even run through brick wall or run into gunfire.

What happens when someone has any one or more of these six Channels, people are more inclined to trust that person in terms of direction. There is almost a blind trust. However, this can also backfire. People might get angry later when they find out later their blind trust wasn't deserved or was abused.

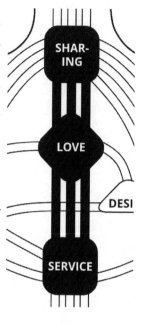

Someone who doesn't have these leadership Channels active has to work harder to convince people, but the advantage is there is a lower chance for disappointment later, because people know why they trust this person.

QUALITIES IN OTHER PEOPLE

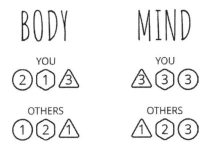

We've already covered the "others" aspect with the Triangles. Let's see what the rest of the symbols reveal. They tell us what qualities we like in other people, what we find attractive in others. If someone has many qualities in "you" that you have in "others", their "attraction" meter on the relationship page goes up. You would also see green LED's light up whenever somebody has the same quality you have marked in the"others" row.

Again, let's use my own example to show you how this works before interpreting a few more celebrities later in the book.

First, we see that I like someone with a Triangle-1 (Success) on both sides as well as a Hexagon-2 (Realist). This means I like people who are happy when they are successful, people who are hard-working and disciplined with body and mind, but also have realistic expectations. I don't like dreamers and I don't like pessimists who constantly worry about things that can go wrong. I prefer people who are confident, but not overconfident.

When we look at the Circles, you can see I like people who have the same number as I have on the mind, a Circle-3 (Initiator). I like people who know what they want and go after it in life. I like people who say what they want, who have a vision, who have expectations in life. But on the body side, it's a different story. We see a Circle-1, which means I prefer people who don't constantly bother me with something. I don't like people who constantly go after other people, but I also don't like Opportunists like myself so much. I prefer someone who waits to be invited, someone who is available but waits to respond or react. People who are constantly pushing and always travelling are generally a little bit too much for me. I prefer "passive" people when it comes to physical action, but "active" ones when it comes to the mind and speaking. I like people who speak up when they have something to say, but don't physically bother people and only do things when somebody wants something.

Ideally, you want other people with the qualities in your "others" row. But you really can't stand when a person not only has a different number from your "others" row but also a different number from "you". This means you don't usually find such people attractive nor are you compatible. Their quality, which is missing from both "you" and "others", is the one you will react worst to.

GOALS

The qualities you like in other people (the six symbols in the "other" row) are actually something you'd like to possess yourself. I tricked you a little bit when I said that the second row in the Graph shows us what kind of people we like. While this is true, actually it's about what we would like to be ourselves. It's about our ambitions.

If you have the goal or desire to change things in your nature, of course you will like people who have these qualities. So the "other" row basically tells us two things: What you would like to be *and* what kind of people you like.

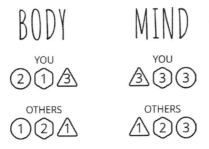

Let's look at my own example again. On the mind side I am a Circle-3 and my goal is a Circle-3 also. That means I don't have the desire to change a thing – on the contrary – I'm perfectly happy the way I interact. I'm happy to be an Initiator who says what he wants when he wants.

Yet, when you look at my Triangles, I will indeed always make "Fun" a priority in life, however I have a desire to be successful given my Triangle-1's in the "others" row. You can interchange the word "others" with "goals". I might not always succeed with this, because the "Fun" theme will always rule my life, but I will make an effort.

Looking at my body side, I wish to be more relaxed with my Circle-1. But I also want to be more courageous with the Hexagon-2 versus the Hexagon-1 that I actually am.

If somebody were to have a Hexagon-3 in "you" and a Hexagon-1 in "others", they would be a fearless/shameless person, but make an effort to be more careful.

LIFE CYCLES

When we look at the data in BaanTu, we see two distinctions. Firstly, the traits that determine your nature and secondly the kinds of environment you are attracted to, what kind of people you would like to be with.

The sum total of your life is the result of these two factors: Who you are and what your environment is. Image yourself floating in space and there is nothing around you. If there is nothing around you, there is nothing to do or to see. So how do you know who you are? Only when you are put in a certain environment will it be possible to reveal parts of you nature. It's the people around you, the life around you, that gives you opportunities to interact.

Two people might have identical traits, but if you place them in different environments, their lives might be totally different. We all know that the environment shapes you, it's an influence, but it also provides you with certain opportunities to live out who you are. At the same time it could deny you to live out certain aspects of you. There are many movies and tales that explore this theme, such as *The Prince and the Pauper* and *Trading Places*.

On the BaanTu page, there is a little panel entitled "Life

Cycles". It has two dates, one for "Repetition" and one for "Mirror". I discovered that some of the themes related to our environment repeat in cycles. These cycles are connected to the Lunar Nodes and last approximately 18.6 years. Every 18.6 years there is a theme in your life that repeats. You can see

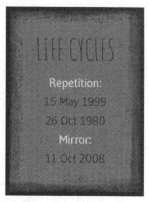

LIFE CYCLES

Repetition:
15 May 1999
26 Oct 1980
Mirror:
11 Oct 2008

this in how your environment treats you and in the quality of places you are in and the kinds of people who turn up or you work with.

Sometimes you have a very challenging period. Sometimes life is "easy" and your environment is friendly. But whatever it is, it will probably repeat every 18.6 years.

Image your life path like train tracks. Sometimes the scenery is picturesque and it's sunny and sometimes it's boring, raining, or storming. The "Repetition" date shows the last two repetitions based on todays' date. When you go back in time and look at these periods in time, they should have something in common in terms of how life is treating you right now. Don't look at the exact day. Rather use broad brush strokes and look at periods of a few months. How was life around that time?

When you look at the dates in-between the repetitions, when you use approximately 9.3 years, this is the Nodal half-cycle. This would be a thematic mirror to how life is treating you right now. You could also say everything is up-side down from what it was then. It's not just a matter of "good" or "bad". Although this might be the case, this would be an oversimplification. You might also see that you were more pessimistic and now you are more optimistic as a result of how life was treating you.

In the Menu of BaanTu is the Life Cycle Calculator. Type in any date and see its repetitions and mirrors. Say there was a life-changing event in the past, maybe you began a new job or moved to a new country. You could type in that date and see when it repeats. It doesn't always repeat in the same way, but whatever it is will make you feel similar.

Life-Cycles Calculator

2005-04-23   YYYY-MM-DD

Calculate

Repetition:	Mirror:
27 Jun 1949	10 Sep 1958
17 Jan 1968	13 Jun 1977
16 Aug 1986	5 Jan 1996
23 Apr 2005	**26 Jul 2014**
16 Dec 2023	13 Feb 2033
12 Jul 2042	24 Nov 2051
31 Jan 2061	24 Jun 2070

The "Mirror" is a good indication of why things happened at a certain time in your life. For example, whatever happens today is largely the result of what you did at the Nodal mirror date, 9.3 years earlier. The Nodal Cycle calculation is very complex, because the Lunar Nodes make strange movements. BaanTu precisely calculates this. So, you might notice that sometimes the Nodes move very quickly and at other times very slowly. One way of looking at the "Mirror" is comparing it to a seed that was planted. It's usually a half Nodal Cycle later that you begin to see the results of what you planted.

GEORGE MICHAEL

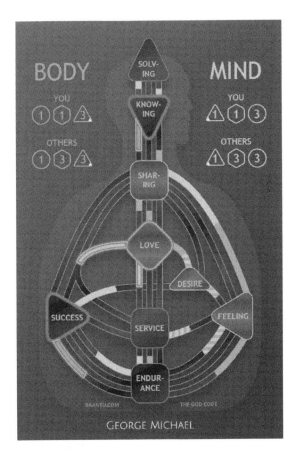

G eorge Michael was an English singer and songwriter who rose to fame as a member of the duo *Wham!* He sold more than 115 million records and was one of the best-selling artists of all time.

I lived near his house in London for ten years, saw him walking down the streets a few times, and knew a few of the people who worked with him. Many years ago I was on the same record label as he was.

I recently saw on television the documentary *Freedom* he was working on shortly before his death. It was completed by his close friend and manager. What you hear about his life and nature confirms a lot of what we can see in BaanTu.

When we look at his Triangles, we see the two things that made him happy and controlled his mood: Success and Feeling. To be precise, he had Success on the mind side and Feeling on the body. That means he judged his ideas and what he said, but also what he wanted to hear from others, by whether it allowed him to succeed in life or not. He had a hard-working mind, but the body side it was a different story. When it came to "doing" he wasn't as hard working and cared more about enjoying himself. His emotions controlled how much and what he was doing, but more importantly, who he was doing it with. If things got physically difficult or unpleasant, he would stop.

The Circle on the mind shows a 3, which made him an Initiator. This really goes with what I know about him. He wanted to be in total control of his career. Some called him a control freak. He even said it about himself. So we know that he aimed high, that he wanted to be in control, and that he wanted to be successful. He wasn't listening to what other people told him to do. He once said in an interview that from the first moment he walked into the office of his record label at the age of 18, he realised that they had no clue how to make him a pop star. Since then, he never did anything they said.

When we look at his Life Gates, we see that Knowing, Success and Love were his primary themes. In a nutshell, this was what his life was about. So the Success theme appears for the second time. He said many times that when he was young he decided he wanted to be famous. Love means he could only do things he loved, and couldn't be with people he didn't care about. That's what made things so difficult with his record label Sony Music when he later fell out with them.

The activated Desire Centre shows he was stubborn, which was confirmed in the documentary by Elton John who said: "George is very stubborn. He is one of the most stubborn people I've met."

You have to understand that not only does he have a defined Desire Centre, he is also an Initiator who doesn't like people telling him what to do.

The thing that caused him the most trouble though, was his double Hexagon-1. It destroyed his life. Some people are more lucky with a Hexagon-1 than others, but once you are traumatized as a double 1, and at the same time extremely exposed to the outside (as you are as a celebrity) it's hard to fully recover.

A Hexagon-1 is not only a Pessimist, but very sensitive. It has very little resilience. These aren't tough people. And you have to be tough to be one the most famous artists in the world. James Cordon said in the film: "George had a layer of skin missing. He bruised easier, which is why he could write these amazing songs."

Michael himself said that when he was at the peak of his career at the age of 25 and the biggest solo artist in the world, he was the most unhappy. He couldn't deal with it. It was not what he wanted. But it was too late to get out.

What began then was a retrieval from the music industry, but when you are the biggest artist with the biggest record company in the world, this isn't going to go down well with some powerful people, who are making a lot of money out of you. He was terribly unhappy and didn't want to promote his music anymore, which led to a huge fight with Sony Music.

George said: "I wanted to be successful, but never wanted to be somebody else." He was hinting about Madonna and other big artists, who he thought created another persona or image to suit the industry. Somebody with a Triangle-2 is much better suited at giving people the image they want. A Triangle-2 is only happy if the other people are happy. They are actors. He didn't have that.

He also said: "I was struggling with having too much attention. Promotion feels like to prostitute yourself."

Even though his mind and what he said was driven by Success, he had a Triangle-3 (Feeling) on the body side, which controlled everything he physically did. He was physically incapable to prostitute himself or live a lie. Again, Triangle-3's don't see the point to be somebody else or to lie. All they want is to feel good so when things get difficult and the fun totally stops, they want to quit.

You ask any artist who was on a long tour and had to promote their album around the world, and you will find out very quickly how hard that kind of life is. It's not glamorous and it isn't fun. It is brutal. It's all the things that a Triangle-3 will eventually have a problem with.

A double Hexagon-1 like George really struggles with being too exposed. Some people are better in dealing with this and controlling the danger, but he wasn't. He didn't even try and got hurt more and more.

The fact that he was gay and couldn't tell anyone also made things a lot worse. You can really see how his Success mind Triangle didn't want to come out and risk his career, but at the same time he was totally uncomfortable to live a lie on the physical side. His low resilience made things worse. On one side, he was afraid of destroying his career, but on the other side, he was deeply unhappy with the career. He was trapped. He couldn't cope.

*

When you look at the body side, you see a double one theme. He was a Reactor (Circle-1), combined with insecurity (Hexagon-1). He was not somebody chasing after other people or pushing them. He was in fact shy and hid. He was waiting for people and things to come to him, despite the fact that he had an Initiator mind. That only made him very outspoken. He would say things whenever he wanted.

Despite the fact that he was a Hexagon-1 on body and mind, he has Hexagon-3's in the "other" row so his goal in life was to be courageous and to overcome his natural shyness and pessimism.

He never was in love or had a partner until he met Anselmo at Rock in Rio in 1991. Anselmo was just a "normal" guy in the crowd staring at him. I told you that Reactors never aim high or have a plan in what they want in life. They let things come to them and this is exactly how he met Anselmo. He said he *waited* a lifetime to be loved. Reactors wait for things to come to them. The body side tells so much about how someone meets people.

With that, a very happy time began in George's life only to be crushed when he found out months later that Anselmo had AIDS. It was another blow to him and took him years to recover from this, at which time his mother died and sent him spiralling again into the next crisis.

The only thing that mattered to him was to enjoy himself and to be successful, but he felt terrible and his career was in ruins after he lost the lawsuit with Sony where he wanted to get out of a contract he called "slavery".

He said: "From the day that I found out about Anselmo to the day I was well on the mend from my mother, I was just in constant fear. I was so spiritually crushed after my mum died and felt so picked on by the gods. I lived in constant fear of death and fear of the next bereavement."

Do you remember when I told you that Hexagon-1's are driven by fear? He had a double Hexagon-1, and when they have traumatic events in their lives, it can become very difficult, up to a point they almost never fully recover. It can make them paranoid. It would be wrong to see this as a general problem though. Some people who are traumatised were meant to change their life and live differently afterwards. Their environment shouldn't pressure them to back to how their life was before. They are making things worse with that.

Everyone in the film said that he was a private person, also something that comes from the Hexagon-1. These people hide. He also had a Circle-1 on the body, so not only did he make it difficult for people to reach him, but he had no interest in going after people either. George was shy and he was waiting for life to hand him things when it came to people. His mind was different. It wanted to be in control, it was stubborn, and also insecure.

He was also known for using a lot of drugs. His few friends were constantly worried. It was his way to cope with the world. Most days he spent sitting in his house eating ice cream and watching something on TV or playing a game while smoking cannabis. Double Hexagon-1's are very private and not very social. They love to stay home and hate crowds.

When you look at his qualities under "others", you can see that he loved people who had big dreams, people who were incredibly confident. The ones who had a Hexagon-3 on both the mind and body. These were the ones who didn't annoy him. Who annoyed him were likely to be the Realists, the ones who always told him that something was wrong with his negativity and pessimism, but also lacked the ability to see the world through rose-coloured glasses. He didn't want people to bring him down to a stark-cold reality. He didn't like "calculating" people. He wanted somebody to either be a bold dreamer, or if he couldn't get that, somebody like himself who was shy, a recluse, and a pessimist.

His own lack of confidence plus trauma is shown in the last words from him in the film, shortly before he died: "I wanted to be remembered for having integrity and my songs. But it's all very unlikely. I think it's been a waste of time. A waste of effort..."

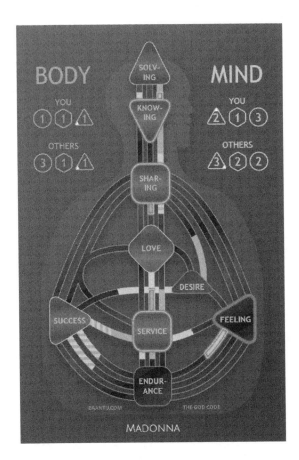

MADONNA

Madonna is another one of the all-time greats in the music business. The reason I picked her Graph was to show how one can have a double Hexagon-1 and still being able to deal with the challenges of being such a public person.

Of course, it's hard for any of us to really know what goes on inside of Madonna. But we know that her level of control verges on the paranoid. She isn't like Taylor Swift who lets her fans close. Madonna keeps everyone at a distance. When she does interviews, nobody is allowed to ask questions that haven't been approved before. She is not a socialite, mixing with other people all the time. She is, in fact, a recluse, possibly surrounding herself with yes-men.

While there are some similarities to George Michael, there is also an enormous difference. What they share is their motivation to be successful. Both of them do indeed need success to be happy. But the difference is George has it on the mind and Madonna on the body. George wants to use his mind for things to succeed, but Madonna her body. She has the ability to physically work hard in a way that George lacked. This is clear in their fitness levels. George was often overweight, struggling to keep his weight, while Madonna is always incredibly fit and in good shape. She was constantly seen jogging or doing intense workouts. Somebody with a Feeling Triangle on the body finds this very difficult.

But I think the biggest difference is Madonna's Triangle-2 on the mind (Respect). She wants to impress everyone. She wants to use her mind to get approval from others. With some people that can become a bit grotesque as they get older. For them it's not enough to retire from the stage with grace after they've made enough money. They need the constant applause and attention. You can see how Madonna makes this huge effort to keep it all going. She is terribly upset if the critics or people in general talk badly about her. With her low resilience, you can see how much this has bothered her during her career.

What she has in common with George is her Initiator mind and Reactor body. She knows what she wants and she goes after it with her mind. She doesn't like to be told what to do with her mind. That goes for her ideas and what she says and also when she says something.

But when it comes to meeting people, she is shy and never pushes someone. It's usually people coming to her, and fame can help with this. At the same time, she isn't available to many people due to her Hexagon-1.

Compared with George, she has one of her Life Gates in Service, which is also permanently defined. This means she is much more commercially orientated. She pays attention to what people want. She has Love-Service, but also Success-Service.

Madonna likes pushy "go-getters" (Initiators) on the body side, she likes to be conquered, while George would have found this annoying. He has a Circle-1 on the body in "others". He preferred people like himself, who are not chasing other people and always on the go. But despite the fact that she likes people who take the initiative physically, one has to see with clear eyes in what ways this has to happen. There is a Hexagon-1. This is the same Hexagon she also has herself on the body side, so this means this is a very black and white thing for her. People are either what she has under "others" and "you" (herself) or they annoy her. There is no middle ground. They can only be compatible *and* attractive, or a nuisance. She can't stand two kinds of people: Overconfident people and Realists. Yes, she likes it when the other people take the initiative, but they also have to act shy, with little confidence, and act sensitively, otherwise she could get uncomfortable very quickly. On the mind side, she prefers realistic thinkers and speakers. Although she has sympathy and understanding for pessimists (she is one herself) and shy speakers, her preference would be for a slightly more confident speaker. But what she really can't stand and the people who probably hurt her the most, the people she would find also insensitive, are the Hexagon-3's. She doesn't like over-optimistic or over-confident thinkers or speakers. She doesn't like dreamers who are unaware of what could go wrong and don't think they have to prepare.

Looking at her goals ("others" row), she wants to overcome her Circle-1 on the body, becoming more pushy and in control (Circle-3), with the Success theme reinforced (Triangle-1). On the mind side, she wants to be a funnier person, more outspoken, but less controlling.

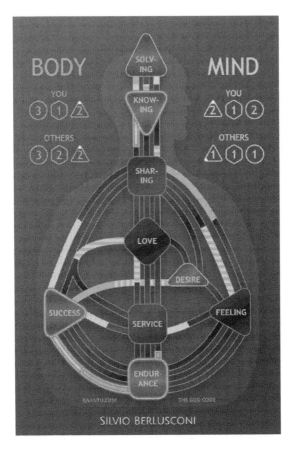

SILVIO BERLUSCONI

I saw the documentary *My Way: The Rise and Fall of Silvio Berlusconi* and having had a birth time for him was another superb opportunity to understand the BaanTu data.

First, we see a 2/3 (mind/body) Circle combination.

I already mentioned that these people can have many affairs in their life. But what it actually means is that they use their bodies to get what they want. Not only did Berlusconi go after all the people he wanted in his life, he also convinced them with his Opportunistic mind.

He began in property sales and said he was extremely good at selling apartments when he had his first company. To understand what drives him and what it's all about for Berlusconi, to understand what makes him happy or miserable, you have to look at his Triangles. Here we see a double Triangle-2. It's all about respect. He wanted to be adored, he wanted to be held in high regard and he cares a lot about what other people think of him.

When I was watching the movie, the first thing I thought was: "I never saw such a show-off in my life!"

Everything he did had only one purpose: He wanted to impress people. Money for him was just a means to impress. He has an enormous villa with over 70 rooms, many of them stuffed to the ceiling with gift, pictures, and memorabilia from other famous people he knows. He has this insane obsession to show everyone how important he is and how all the other important people like and adore him, by collecting and showcasing all the gifts and personal notes they've sent him and the rewards they've given him. His life is nothing but a big trophy collection (including his wives).

But then you look at his double Hexagon-1 and the

198

need to impress reaches a new dimension. You could see his incredible insecurity. This man wanted to go after people, but he was shy and insecure. Of course, money, fame, and all the other things he collected to impress people, helped him deal with his insecurities.

Everything in his life was built on a lie. Even his hair is fake. Triangle-2 people are the best actors. But he wasn't stupid. He went university and studied law. This fits perfectly with his Life Gate in Knowing. He had to know things, but he was also somebody who spends a lot of time "Solving" things, because he has Solving defined. You might argue that he "solved" a lot of problems for the mafia, also benefitting himself and giving him the resources to get started in the property business.

Then we see a defined Desire Centre, making him stubborn, as well as the Life Gates in Success and Endurance, which need no further explanation to understand what this man's life was about.

The thing that puzzled me at first was why he gave the film makers access to interviews and allowed them to film him after his reputation was ruined following all the corruption and sex scandals with underage girls in his villa. The courts ruled him guilty. All he could do was to embarrass himself more with this film.

If anyone else had that kind of money, they would probably just disappear from the public eye and enjoy life. But he wanted to tell his story, which in hindsight made things even worse. Because his reputation is ruined, he is in a bad mood. None of his money will help. If he had Triangle-1's instead of Triangle-2's, he would have no problem. But because of his double Respect theme, he made a desperate attempt to fix his reputation by giving the filmmakers access. And it made things worse. It showed everyone what kind of a person he really is. When he saw the finished film he was furious, because he assumed the film maker would glorify him, which he didn't.

You could also see all these people in the background, hovering around to make sure nothing would happen to make him look bad. He is so paranoid that he employs tons of people looking out for him or shielding him.

Despite always going after people and girls, he is private. With his double Hexagon-1, he totally controls who has access to him and who doesn't. You can't get near him, even if you wanted. But you also can't criticise him or ask unapproved questions. Everyone has to follow his "script". You can see all the yes-men around him.

His undefined Centres in the Graph give an idea what doesn't matter to him. Sharing, Love, Service, and Feeling. It's not there. He doesn't give a damn what people want, he is not in the business of making them feel good, and he isn't a sharing person.

*

When you look at Berlusconi's Hexagons under "others", you see one thing right away. He doesn't like overconfident people or dreamers. He doesn't like people who are unprepared and don't see danger. He doesn't have a Hexagon-3 himself, and he also doesn't find it attractive. There is no Hexagon-3 anywhere. Therefore this are also the people who are most likely to annoy him, with what he would call insensitivity.

Looking at his goals and ambitions ("others" row), he has no regrets about his behaviour and certainly no intention to tone down his pushiness on the body side. He also has a reinforced Respect theme, while on the mind side he makes an effort to succeed and to be more passive.

DONALD TRUMP

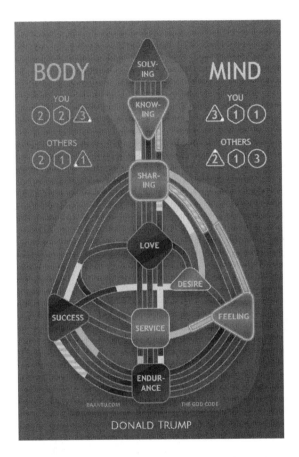

D onald Trump is a very unusual president, because he
is not a career politician. In BaanTu, the part that
shows him to be an atypical politician is his double Fun
Triangle-3. With most politicians, there is a mix of either

Success or Respect in the Triangles. The fact that Trump has many Channels defined (he doesn't need other people to feel motivated) plus a defined Desire Centre makes him not a big team player and also stubborn. All these traits are not helpful for a career in politics, where you depend on the support and teamwork of others.

Trump was different, because he didn't need financial backing or party support to run a campaign. He had his own money. This made it possible for somebody with his configuration to even have a chance at politics.

Because he has a lot of Feeling defined, not just in the Triangles but also the Pressure Centre where his Life Gate sits, he is someone who wears his emotions on his sleeve. He is deeply driven by the way he feels. All his reactions are emotionally based. He does whatever makes him feel good. He is not primarily motivated to succeed or by what other people think about him. He wants to enjoy himself. Nothing else. The lack of the Triangle-2 (Respect) is really evident with him. He couldn't care less what others think about him. He's not into upholding any image about the office or "acting" Presidential. He's going to say or tweet what he wants if it makes him feel good.

Looking at his Circle 1/2 combination (mind/body), he is not a very pushy person. His mind waits to be invited and he uses his body only to go after real opportunities. He is not a man driven by a vision. He is also not a confident speaker (Hexagon-1). When you look at his policies, most of what he does is an emotional Reaction. It doesn't matter if it's North Korea, ISIS, or China taking away jobs from America. He reacts to everyone and everything that makes him feel bad. He wants to build a wall at the Mexican border, because he feels bad some American people suffer through illegal immigration.

His Hexagon-1 on the mind side means that he is very sensitive and easily hurt. When you look at what kind of people he prefers, you see that he also wants people with a Hexagon-1, who are sensitive when they speak. He can't stand rude people.

His Life Gates are connected to Sharing, Knowing, and Feeling. These are the most important themes in his life. He wants to share things with the collective to make people and himself feel good. But he also likes to know things and be informed.

On the body side, which controls his actions and the people he would like to meet, we see the theme of the Opportunist (Circle-2) and the Realist (Hexagon-2). When he acts, he is very realistic about the dangers involved, but he only acts when he sees an opportunity. He is neither constantly attacking nor waiting for things to come his way. He is waiting for the right moment and person to turn up before making his move. His physical confidence falls in the medium, in the middle, neither too much nor too little. While he likes people who are Initiators on the mind side, people with a vision and who go after it, he is somebody who prefers to be asked when it comes to speaking instead of being outspoken.

On the body side, he likes people like himself. He likes the Opportunist, but compared to him, he prefers them a little more shy and less confident. He likes pessimistic people who have a good sense of all the things that could go wrong, but he also likes people that can work hard and don't quit when things get difficult.

What he can't stand are people who are physically overconfident and who are using their bodies to be pushy with other people (Circle-3), or the other extreme, people who wait for life to knock at their door (Circle-1), being too passive. He doesn't like people who use their minds just to succeed (Triangle-1). It's the one number he doesn't have anywhere in his Triangles. Not in "you" and not in "others". Because he has Sharing and Feeling in the Life Role, you can see why he loves to tweet. He is constantly sharing with the people his feelings, but he also want to make Americans feel better.

His own ambitions ("others" row) are to be more respected and successful, instead of just having fun (Triangle-1 and Triangle-2), and to also to say things when he likes, instead of waiting to be asked – in a nutshell, to be more in control with his mind (Circle-3).

VLADIMIR PUTIN

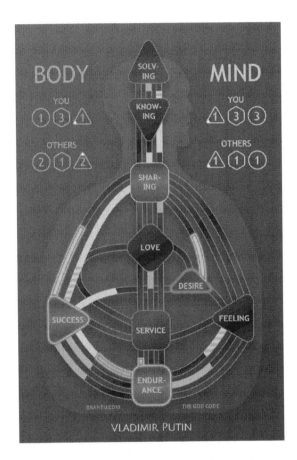

C ompared with Trump, here we have someone who has a vision. He knows what he wants and he goes after it (Circle-3). The biggest difference though is that Putin is the "classic" politician. We have a very strong

Success theme that appears twice in the Triangles, once in the Pressure Centres, and also in the Life Gates. He also has one of his Life Gates in an always defined Endurance Centre, plus he has a very thick skin and is confident on both the mind and body. You can't intimidate such a man. He isn't afraid of anything. He's neither running away from physical threats nor running away from an argument. At the same time, he has two Hexagon-1's on the "other" row, so he makes an effort to be careful and not to be too rude. He is also making an effort to tone down his pushy mind, but to be more active on the body side.

When you look at his data on **baantu.com**, you can also see that this man is a team player. This is another thing that's very important in politics. He isn't as stubborn as Trump, because his Desire Centre is undefined. Despite the fact that he uses his mind to get what he wants, he doesn't physically go after people and bother them (Circle-1 body). He lets them come to him. He is a Reactor when using his body. He makes himself available. But when it comes to his ideas, what he says, and using his mind, he doesn't need an invitation. He is outspoken. He has a big mouth. He can be rude. He will interrupt you. I also think that you won't easily find a more competitive person than Putin. This man wants to win.

Looking at his data, we can see that he doesn't like Realists. He himself is an Optimist on both mind and body, and the people he likes should be shy Pessimists.

You could also say that he likes people who are sensitive and have great awareness of all the things that could go wrong. He finds Realists boring. Putin is a dreamer, he thinks big, and he isn't afraid of anything. You could also say that sometimes he behaves slightly insensitively.

In the film about Silvio Berlusconi, one could see that Putin liked Berlusconi and supported him often. Berlusconi has, of course, some qualities that Putin is looking for in other people. He has a double Hexagon-1 and a Triangle-2 on the body. Putin likes people who do things in order to be respected.

When you look at Putin's and Berlusconi's relationship data on **baantu.com**, Berlusconi however disliked everything about Putin. But since he was the president of Russia and Putin actually liked Berlusconi, he wouldn't show it or tell. He was just using it to boast. Don't forget Berlusconi is a good actor, like all Triangle-2's. He used Putin to show the whole world what great friends they are. Putin became another "trophy" for Berlusconi, who has that double Triangle-2 (Respect).

Putin has one of his Life Gates in an undefined Desire Centre. Although he isn't always stubborn, he can be, depending on the situation. But you could also view this as a man with principles who knows how to say "no". In order to do that, he needs the right partner or Transit. His Life Role is defined by Success, Endurance, and Desire. This alone tells you a lot about how he got to the position he has today. His open mind Centres, with no Life Gates also tell you that he isn't an intellectual or interested in figuring out solutions. He's more of a "doer", less of a "thinker".

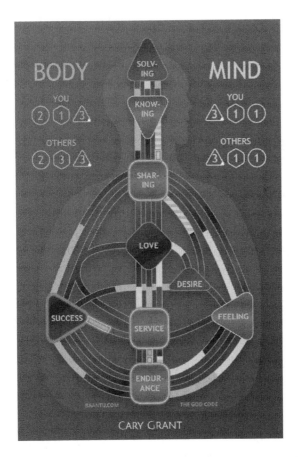

Here we have another double Hexagon-1. This is more proof that somebody who is insecure and shy can be very successful. I've already said that it's a fallacy to assume only over-confident people do well. I might even go so far as to say that some insecure people can be more driven to succeed because of their insecurities.

The reason I chose him is, again, because of a new movie about his life *Becoming Cary Grant*. With his data in the **baantu.com** database, I was curious if what I'd learn about his life would match what we see. It's often very hard for us to judge an actor by the roles they play and movies they make. It doesn't tell you a lot about who they are. In fact, their roles can be misleading and hide who they actually are. Sometimes after they die, you get to hear much more about them.

It was the director Howard Hawks who helped shape the movie star, Cary Grant. He sensed a fascinating insecurity in Grant, combined with humour. Before that, Grant was only cast for his good looks, had little lines to speak, and his characters were dull.

He was originally from Bristol, England. After he was expelled from school (which doesn't surprise me with his two Fun Triangles), he joined the Pender Troupe, honing his acting skills. School was clearly not his idea of having fun. The Pender Troupe later travelled to the United States, performing in New York's Hippodrome, the largest theatre in the world at the time. He then decided to stay in the US and the rest is history. The body Circle-2 saw an opportunity. Grant was not an Initiator, but when the right opportunity came along, he would act. As a 2/1 Circle he was not pushy. This was a patient and well-behaved man.

He had a double Hexagon-1, which made him shy and sensitive. He was traumatized (as can happen with Hexagon-1's) by events from his childhood and was in long psychiatric treatment, using LSD. You could see that some parts of his childhood left deep marks and were not forgotten. Things from the past can cast a long shadow into the future of a Hexagon-1. It shapes them. It has a huge effect.

It was said in the movie that he was a lone figure, private. He didn't like crowds and wasn't a party-goer. His daughter said that one would imagine they were out at parties and premiers, but instead they were at home watching TV, playing cards, or backgammon.

His last wife, Barbara Jaynes, said that he was shy and anxious at first that she was the right person. Hexagon-1's can have trust issues. She also said that he didn't like to be in the public and he hated when he had to give a public speech. On occasions when he had to, he wouldn't eat and was terribly nervous beforehand.

Later in life he had a TV show *Conversations with Cary Grant* that he loved because people could ask him questions and he would respond with a joke after looking at some of his old movie clips.

As a Reactor mind, he loved it when people asked questions. That's what a Reactor is good at. They are like a well that people drink from. They make themselves available. Triangle-3 minds are often funny. In his case, we had a double-fun person, highly sensitive, but shy and private.

When you look at his Life Gates, we see that Sharing, Success, Endurance, and Service are highlighted. But we also see a Channel formed between Endurance and Service. He was in tune with what people wanted, but also he would not easily give up an endeavour even if he failed. Of course, Sharing and Success don't need much of an explanation if you've shared your work with the whole world and were one of the most successful actors on the planet.

What's interesting when looking at his data is the similarity between the "you" and the "others" row. Everything is the same, with the exception of the Hexagon on the body. While we know he preferred people who were more courageous and fearless than he was, he also made a big effort to be more courageous himself – to believe in his physical abilities and to be less shy.

Looking at the two Hexagon-1's on the mind ("you" and "others"), it's obvious that he didn't like rudeness or people who interrupt or bother others. He liked patient Circle-1's who wait to be asked.

Double Triangle-3's like him are always at risk of dropping out of school (like he actually did) when it isn't fun. In fact, if he couldn't do things that were fun or made him feel good, he would be in a bad mood. No amount of money or prestige could make up for this. They would always come second. And he had no time for people who were vain (Triangle-2) or would sell their grandmother in order to succeed (Triangle-1).

THE BECKHAMS

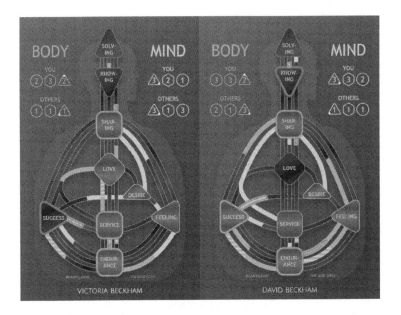

Here we come to one of the world's best-known celebrity couples. Their marriage has stood the test of time, which isn't surprising when you look at their five-star relationship rating below.

While a high star rating is no guarantee of a lasting relationship, the chances are a lot better. I do remember when I first released the **baantu.com** relationship page with the star ratings. Back then, Brad Pitt and Angelina Jolie were still together and held the Beckham's place as the most followed couple. It's seems that they were the

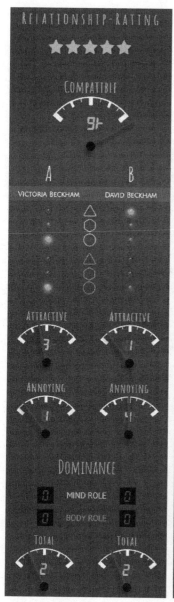

Poster Couple, but BaanTu gave them a zero-star rating. People told me that there must be something wrong with my calculation. But when they announced they were separating a year later to the sheer surprise of nearly everyone, it was me who smiled and said "I told you so."

The thing that stands out with the Beckhams' is that they have a very high compatibility but not very high attractions. This can make the relationship a little bit boring, but it works well.

At the beginning of their marriage, there were a few scandals in the tabloids about David's affairs. When you look at David's data, we see of course our old friend the 2/3 (mind/body) Circle combination. The big seducers of the world. Not only that, he also has a double Hexagon-3, which makes him the most confident person on the planet. He isn't shy about his body and he isn't ashamed when he speaks. Looking at Victoria's data in "others", you can see David's confidence and his way of going after others really annoy her, explaining all the red LED's on his side.

So why did they choose each other? When David met Victoria, she was at the pinnacle of her career with the Spice Girls. They were one of the most famous pop bands in the world at the time. David was only known in footballer circles, she only as member of the Spice girls. What they both have is a Triangle-2. They want to be famous and respected. The moment they started dating, they went from well-known to celebrity superstars, which must have made them both very happy.

The other aspects that are strong in their relationship is the "additional motivation". These two can get a lot more done in life when they are together. But you can also see that these two are not "thinkers". They don't "talk" more, they "do" more. They have a high community motivation, which of course is also family. This explains why they wanted a lot of children. They are motivated to spend a lot of time with the family. David already had a lot of "community" in his own data, which is only compounded with Victoria. Of course, a football club is another form of a community. David needs to be close with people in his life. He needs his daily dose of a community. He probably couldn't function well alone on a desert island.

Their dominance is relatively low. I always call dominance the silent relationship killer. A level of two is not a huge problem. But most importantly, we see that one person isn't dominating the other more.

Victoria gives David a big boost in his Life Role by activating two of his Life Gates. They also have two "leadership" Channels when together, which makes them more popular and explains why people have a tendency to follow them.

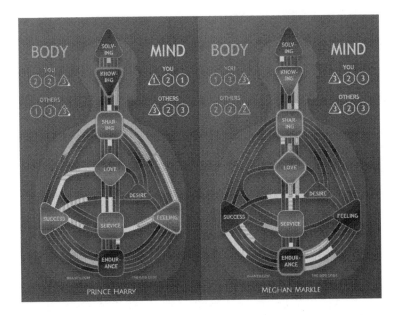

While I was finishing the book, they both announced their engagement via the BBC, also giving a long interview to the British broadcaster. I was, of course, curious to see their data in BaanTu. The fact that Meghan is American, coming from quite a simple background and mixed race makes her an unusual choice for a Royal.

Looking at their relationship data, it becomes clear why Prince Harry goes to all that "trouble". I haven't seen anyone yet with all six LED's lit up, like Meghan has with Harry. She ticks all the boxes. He said he knew almost

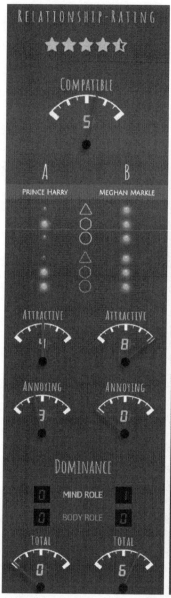

right away that she is "the one".

Their star rating is also high. Four and 1/2 stars. But Harry can annoy Meghan a bit, judging from the "annoying" meter, but we also see, and this is probably worse, that Meghan dominates Harry. To make matters worse, she dominates one of his Life Gates. Dominance is usually overlooked at the beginning of a relationship, but after a while it really starts to bother the one being dominated. This could be felt longer term, and when Harry "snaps" one day, maybe years into the future, she will probably have no idea where any of that is coming from all of a sudden. That's how dominance works, especially if it's so one-sided as in this case.

But all in all, it's an extremely easy relationship. Compatibility is solid as is just about every other aspect. They'll be able to spend a lot of time together. This one could last for quite a while.

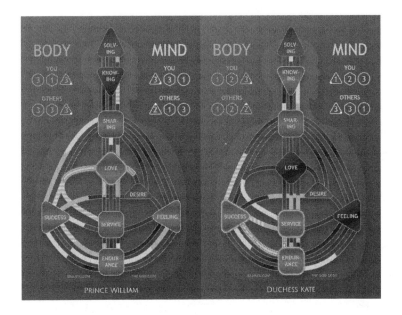

This is a tricky one. It reminds me a bit of Prince Charles and Diana (which we will analyse afterwards), but not quite that bad.

Looking at Kate's data, one can see that family is very important with two Channels from the Communal Circuit, explaining all the children they have. This might initially help gloss over the issues that this relationship has.

This relationship can only survive if they give each other plenty of space. But that is a problem when you are a Royal, because you usually spend a lot of time together.

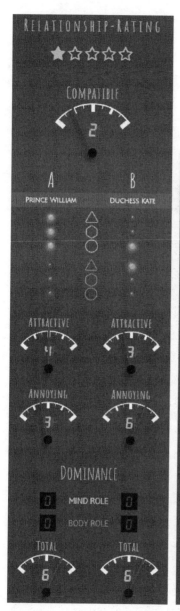

The most glaring challenge of the relationship is the lack of compatibility. They don't really understand each other. While there is a little bit of an attraction between them (which is usually something that jump-starts a relationship), there is a nasty hangover waiting for them after the honeymoon and child-rearing are over.

First of all, we can see that both of them dominate the other quite a lot. It's a mistake to assume when two people dominate each other equally, it cancels out. It doesn't at all. It means it's bad for both sides.

Kate is also more annoying and less attractive (in term of her qualities, not looks) to William. The strains of the relationship will be felt stronger on his side, especially since William is a double Feeling Triangle and nothing is more important than to enjoy himself. He has no interest in acting for an audience, and probably finds the pomp and circumstance surrounding his official roles claustrophobic. It explains why he ditched an official Royal function once to party with his friends, après-ski, in Switzerland. He is probably more outspoken, aggressive, or even rude with his Hexagon-3 on the mind than the public would be aware of. While she is the Initiator when it comes to speaking in the relationship, he is in control when it comes to doing (body Circle).

The positive aspect of the relationship is their increased motivation when they are together, but this is almost worthless when you have such low compatibility.

You start highly motivated to do something together, but every time one person says A the other says B. Or one person makes a suggestion and the other thinks: "Why on earth, out of all the possible choices, would you do that?"

Welcome to the world of relationships. If it's some comfort to you, go and read the quote at the beginning of the book again.

PRINCE CHARLES & DIANA

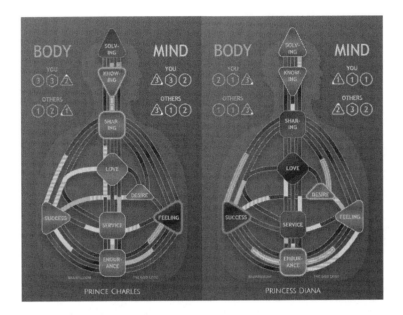

This is one of these relationships, at least on paper, that makes you think: "What did these two people see in each other when they got together?"

But we now know it was pretty much an arranged marriage, and the zero-star rating reflects how this Royal relationship unfolded so miserably in the public eye. It couldn't get much worse. It was almost impossible for them to spend any time together without feeling uncomfortable or having an argument. They were not too compatible, which means they didn't understand each other.

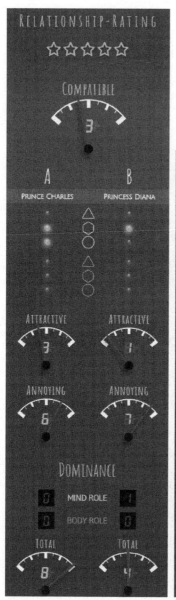

What stands out in their relationship is the almost total lack of attraction Charles had for Diana, and to make matters worse, the incredibly high annoyance coming from her. Charles was slightly more attractive and slightly less annoying for Diana, but all in all, it was still bad.

The dominance coming from Charles is extremely high. I don't know many relationships that could survive that. And although the dominance coming from Diana is lower, she unfortunately dominated one of his Life Gates, which must have been terribly upsetting for him. Despite the fact that they were motivated to do a few things together (although just a little), it wouldn't work with all the incompatibility, dominance, and annoyance present.

Charles was pushier in the relationship with his higher Circles. He was also incredibly confident, both with body and mind, which means Diana, who had a double Hexagon-1 was incredibly sensitive and easily hurt by him. I think it's highly possible that the public role traumatized her, similar to George Michael, who couldn't cope with his double Hexagon-1 and the high level of attention either. She even spoke to him over the phone a few times when she was in trouble. I guess they could relate to each other.

Both Charles and Diana have a Triangle-2, which means they might have put on an act for far too long. It's easy to assume that both of them were better off when this chapter of a relationship that never was one was finally closed.

PRINCE CHARLES & CAMILLA

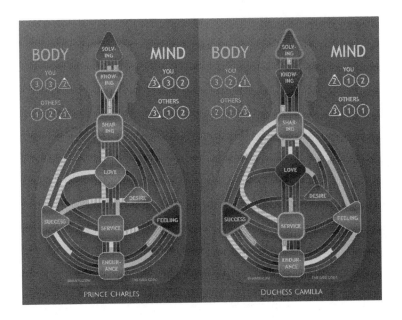

The difference between Charles and Diana and this relationship couldn't be more startling. It leaps from a zero-star relationship to a full five-star relationship.

While it must have felt like day and night to Charles, you must understand that no relationship is perfect. They both might have five stars, but you can still see the weaknesses in this relationship.

Their compatibility is relatively low and you can see that Camilla find Charles' qualities less attractive, some of them downright annoying.

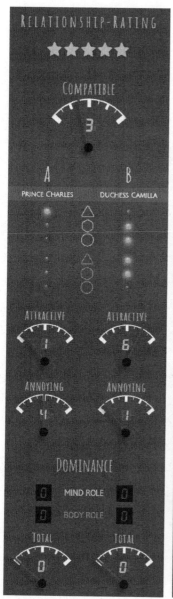

Relationship-Rating

★★★★★

Compatible

3

A
Prince Charles

B
Duchess Camilla

Attractive
1

Attractive
6

Annoying
4

Annoying
1

Dominance

	MIND ROLE	
0	MIND ROLE	0
0	BODY ROLE	0

Total
0

Total
0

Additional Motivation
(for doing things together)

	MIND ROLE	
1	MIND ROLE	0
0	BODY ROLE	0

Total
14

Mental
2

Physical
7

Creativity
9+

Leadership
2

Success
6

Feeling
0

Collective
5

Community
0

232

But what's really excellent in this relationship is the total lack of any dominance. Dominance is usually the driving force for any deep resentments that start to build up over time.

They also have an extremely high motivation to do things together, and because they don't dominate each other, it can be quite enjoyable.

Camilla might not find Charles as attractive as he does with her, but he provides her with an extra motivation for her Life Role, which isn't bad at all. Apart from that, Camilla has a Triangle-2 and she surely must enjoy the Respect she gets as a Royal.

Similar to Diana, Charles lack of sensitivity might bother her occasionally. Although she is not a double Hexagon-1 like Diana and is a little bit tougher, she prefers people with a double Hexagon-1. She likes sensitive people, which Charles isn't. Charles is probably sometimes totally oblivious to just how insensitive and hurtful his actions can be at times.

I'm also sure that Charles is a funny guy (Triangle-3 mind) and Camilla likes funny people, because she has a Triangle-3 in "others" on her mind side.

CHECKING THE BIRTH TIME

When you enter your birth data, you also have to enter a place. The actual place is irrelevant for the calculation of BaanTu. The reason why we need it is because NASA publishes the position of the planets relative to UTC (similar to Greenwich Mean Time). So in order to know where the planets were at your time of birth, we first have to convert your time to UTC. We have to look up the time zone rules for your country at the time you were born. We have to see what the time difference to UTC was. It's also important to know whether there was daylight saving time in place or not. When you enter a place, it's enough to enter the nearest city from your place of birth that was in the same time zone.

In the past, there have been a few providers for the time zone data, which was mainly used by early astrology software. The problem with them was that they sometimes had conflicting or incorrect information about certain places at certain times. Lately we have the IANA, which maintains a time zone database (tz database). This is a collaborative compilation of information about the world's time zones, primarily intended for use with computer programs and operating systems. It isn't perfect either, but it's the best database that exists. For example, we have countries that constantly change their time zone rules. Some of them even create new zones by splitting an existing one into two, while others merge two time zones into one. You can see how difficult it is to maintain and calculate all that historical data. In the last 50 years, Russia alone has one of the most changes in the world with its time zone data. It's almost impossible to keep track of everything. There are still a few places like

Kazakhstan, Russia, even Texas (pre-1970) and a few other places in the US (pre-1970) that can show an incorrect UTC time for your locally entered time.

It's always a good idea to double check the UTC time shown in red under the [GO] button to see if the IANA tz database correctly converted your local time to UTC. In our example above, you can see that the local time was entered at 9:40 AM for Berlin, Germany. We see that UTC is showing at 8:40, which seems to be correct, assuming that there was no daylight savings time in place at the time.

The next step is to verify when your BaanTu data begins to change. Let's say you have a birth time of 16:30. What if BaanTu had a big change at 16:29? The first thing you want to find out are any changes when going backwards and forwards in time from the time you have entered.

Left and right of the [SAVE][GO] buttons, you can see a backward and forward button. When you press backward, BaanTu looks for the next change backwards in time. Once it has found one, you hear the sound of a bell and it will highlight the data that has changed. This doesn't work in the relationship mode. You have to be in single person mode. On the [EASY] page, you see any text that has changed, highlighted. On the [GRAPH] page you see any of the 12 symbols and their numbers highlighted, in case they've changed. When you look at your birth date, you can also see at what time data changed.

If you would like to know what that data was earlier, you could press the button for the other direction (forward in our example) and it will show you what the data was a minute before. You can press the backward button several times again and it will always stop when it finds another change.

To go back to your originally entered birth time, press [GO]. Next, you could check the other direction, in our example this would be going forward. At any point, you can always overwrite the existing data with the new one by pressing [SAVE].

Depending on how reliable your birth time is and depending on how close to the time there are changes, you might want to exclude some of the data from your analysis or at least question it.

Let's assume your birth time is 9:40 and you realise that a Triangle changes from 2 to 1 at 9:38. So we know that this person either has a Respect or Success theme. Despite the fact that in most cases I have a tendency to assume someone was born earlier than later (a nurse might look at the clock *after* the baby was born), you can't assume that this is the case. When the person in question is yourself or somebody you know, it might be possible to find out what is more important in their lives. Does it matter what other people think and say about them or do they just want to succeed, sometimes even despite what everyone else might say or think?

If you can't tell for sure, there is something else you can do. You can say at least that this person is not a Triangle-3. It's not about Feeling. You can at least narrow it down a little. Some people go to an astrologer for their birth time rectification, which I'm not a big fan of. This is very unreliable and usually when you go to several astrologers, they give you several totally different times.

When you want to use somebody's data with BaanTu, you should really be in possession of a birth time with a guaranteed accuracy down to at least +/- 30 minutes, otherwise the value of the information deteriorates quickly. I wouldn't recommend using somebody's data, if you don't have a time of birth. All the celebrities in the BaanTu database have a relatively trustworthy source for their birth time. We don't store anybody without this. Still, there is never any guarantee that the time is 100% accurate.

I always say to people, if you don't recognise anything BaanTu shows you, don't trust it. Trust what you actually see in people and yourself first. BaanTu can only be a tool that helps you to see things clearer in somebody's nature, but it should never be blindly trusted.

This gives you an idea how long a Gate, Circle, Hexagon or Triangle stays the same before changing to the next:

Gate	5.7 days
Circle	~2 days
Hexagon	7.6 hours
Triangle	76 minutes

CONCLUSION

Let's just remind ourselves what BaanTu is and what it isn't. It's also a question that others might ask you occasionally and it's good to have an answer.

BaanTu is built on the understanding that a larger Program is organising all life, which is best understood by imagining the universe as a living being. There is a building plan, but instead of the idea of a central higher being or force, it is shattered into countless aspects of dark matter that we call "Bhan Crystals" in BaanTu.

Every life form on Earth carries two Bhan Crystals and every cell carries one Bhan Crystal. For example, every human carries one Bhan for the mind, influencing what you say and think, and another Bhan for the body, influencing how you physically use your body – what you do.

Despite the fact that life forms are autonomous, they are also influenced. We teach ourselves and learn throughout our life times. We become more intelligent, but there is a greater Program influencing us too, so everything is organised into a larger organism. We carry out many more tasks without knowing that we do. This is similar to cells inside our own bodies that would not understand what their actual task is.

BaanTu comes with the understanding that a human being has certain freedoms in life, but at the same time many things in its nature cannot be changed. If a constant influence is present by the Program, nobody is saying you can't be different, but you are fighting an uphill battle. It's never going to be as easy as it is for the people who the Program wants them to be like this.

BaanTu offers a better understanding of your own strengths and limitations. What the Program wants from you is of course part of your nature, but it's a part of your nature that's not easy to change. With BaanTu, you can have a clearer understanding of it.

BaanTu is not a moralistic system and can't tell you what is "good" or "bad". It can't tell you what to do in life. This is your own responsibility and life. The Program is already supporting you so you can make the right choices.

We all find out where life is taking us by living it. There are many paths to Rome and BaanTu offers you a magnifying glass into your own and other people's pathways. It can reveal what motivates you, and what is responsible for your mood. BaanTu is not about having more happiness. This isn't possible. It's about understanding how you tick and to see that we are all different.

It's also not about how to be like everyone else. There is no human "ideal" that should be chased. We are not meant to be lemmings. You are already what the Program want you to be, but you are also a "work in progress". Don't assume that something is wrong with you and you have to re-invent yourself.

We never know what's next. Life never stands still. It doesn't matter if you are a Initiator full of dreams who has a very strong idea about the future, so long as you understand that the future might always be something different. We only can control it to a certain degree. It's like a cow grazing. It can roam about as much as it likes, but eventually there will probably be an electric fence or a rancher, limiting and corralling its freedom.

Next time you get hurt in life, don't immediately see it as a mistake. If you can't fix it, life maybe doesn't want you to go there. Be smart. Look at the signs. It's the same with relationships. It's wonderful what we can see with BaanTu, but what we don't do is tell you who the right person is. All we can see is why you want to spend more or less time with someone. But even when you have five stars, it doesn't always mean this is the right person. Yet, should they become part of your life, it would be easier for you to spend more time with them. Ultimately, the decision about who is the right person for you is yours, but it doesn't mean you can make it happen. You can only go along, where life is taking you already.

If you are a parent and have a one-star relationship with your child, don't feel bad about it. It only means that this relationship will need space. Don't feel guilty about it and force yourself onto your child. Your child will probably give you signs anyway that it has had "enough" from you after a while. This is not your fault or a problem.

It's a mistake to think we are in total control of our lives and that we can change our nature to anything we like. We create a lot of suffering in people with this unproven assumption. Nobody talks about the millions of people who didn't succeed, instead we celebrate the tiny few who were "lucky". They take credit for something when there is no credit due. It's usually people like them who write books about how you can be like them and go on TV shows to play with the hopes of people, getting even richer by creating more misery. I'm not against someone sharing their story or giving you a few tips. But it's criminal to tell people that they can become *anything* they want, as long as they try hard enough or follow somebody's (paid) advice. These arrogant people might as well tell everyone who didn't make it that they are a total loser.

Everyone who is alive on this planet is needed for whatever reason and in ways we cannot understand. It's not about having the most influence and the most amount of fame or money. This is no indication that the universe needs you more. This universe is not the first or last or only one out there. If life doesn't need something, it gets rid of it. It's brutal. So the fact that you exist means that you are essential for the universe's survival right now. Some people might just be the salt, but we all know how important the right seasoning is for the perfect meal. Everything matters, even if it doesn't to society.

What BaanTu is trying to tell you is that nobody is like you and nobody knows what's best for you. What's even more important is the fact that you are not alone. There is a larger Program looking out for you at every step of your life, despite the fact that it's sometimes down to you to figure some things out.

In the end, no one on this planet will be more happy than another person. So whatever possessions and trophies you might have acquired, you haven't been more happy, more loved, or more important. One day, all of us will be dust and none of these things will matter. We all go back to the same dust where we came from.

Live your life and let it surprise you by what the next day will bring. Sometimes it brings pain to your doorstep, but it's only out of pain that the possibility of pleasure can arise, otherwise we would be dead. And we all will be dead soon enough. So let us celebrate who we are and live it as good as we can for as long as we can. One day at a time.

baantu.com

ABOUT THE AUTHOR

Steve Rhodes is the founder of BaanTu. He is a British musician, computer programmer, book author, and owner of a record company. Born in Austria, he studied mechanical engineering-management before moving to London. While at university, he won a nationwide search for best music-newcomer and subsequently got signed to CBS Records. Various TV, radio, and other media appearances followed. Until 2010, Steve owned one of the leading recording studios in London, Alpha Centauri, which was used by U2, Kanye West, M.I.A., and Depeche Mode. His music can be heard at marquii.net.